MANAGING SUCCESSFUL TEAMS

BUSINESS & MANAGEMENT

MANAGING SUCCESSFUL TEAMS

How to get the results you want by
working effectively with others

John Humphries

How To Books

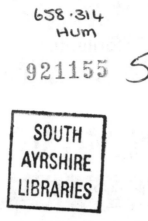

Cartoons by Mike Flanagan

British Library Cataloguing in Publication Data

A catalogue record for this book is available from the British Library

First published by How To Books Ltd, 3 Newtec Place,
Magdalen Road, Oxford OX4 1RE, United Kingdom.
Tel: (01865) 793806. Fax: (01865) 248780.
email: info@howtobooks.co.uk
www.howtobooks.co.uk

First published 1998
Second impression 1999

Note: The material contained in this book is set out in good faith for general
guidance and no liability can be accepted for loss or expense incurred as a result of
relying in particular circumstances on statements made in the book.
The laws and regulations are complex and liable to change, and readers
should check the current position with the relevant authorities before making
personal arrangements.

Cover design Shireen Nathoo Design
Cover image PhotoDisc
Produced for How To Books by Deer Park Productions.
Typeset by Anneset, Weston-super-Mare, North Somerset.
Printed and bound by Cromwell Press, Trowbridge, Wiltshire.

Contents

Acknowledgements   8

Preface   9

1 **Defining a team**   11
   Defining groups and teams   11
   Recognising a successful team   11
   Benefiting from teams   12
   Understanding different types of teams   13
   Case studies   14
   Summary   15

2 **Leading the team**   16
   Understanding how people become leaders   16
   Defining leadership qualities   17
   Assessing the roles and responsibilities of a leader   19
   Looking at different leadership styles   21
   Understanding situational leadership   24
   Identifying influences on leadership style   25
   Case studies   26
   Summary   27
   Exercises   27

3 **Teambuilding**   28
   Questions before you begin   28
   Identifying strengths and weaknesses   30
   Identifying team roles   32
   Allocating roles   34
   Building the team   34
   Case studies   36
   Summary   37

4 **Teamworking**   38
   Understanding the benefits of teamwork   39
   Creating the right environment   39
   Clarifying the objectives   40
   Sharing information   40
   Leading by example   40
   Motivating   40
   Involving   41
   Welcoming ideas   42
   Training   42
   Encouraging the team to perform well   43
   Making meetings worthwhile   43
   Offering opportunities to bond   44
   Case studies   44
   Summary   45

5 **Communicating with your team**   46
   Identifying the purposes of communication   46
   Analysing the causes of communication breakdowns   47
   Identifying communication behaviours   48
   Using the right words, tone and body language   51
   Being assertive   52
   Giving instructions   53
   Improving listening skills   54
   Case studies   55
   Summary   56

6 **Handling discontent within the team**   57
   Analysing the causes   57
   Dealing with the symptoms   59
   Case studies   62
   Summary   62

7 **Training the team**   64
   Comparing the types of training available   64
   Deciding what training is required   66
   Planning the training   67
   Preparing the training session   67
   Delivering the training exercises   67
   Assessing the training   68
   Keeping a record   68
   Case studies   69
   Summary   70

8 **Assessing your team** 71
   Monitoring your team 71
   Involving your team 72
   Getting your team to appraise each other 73
   Case studies 73
   Summary 74

Appendix 1 Team Exercises 75
   1 What Time Is It? 76
   2 The Tower Project 78
   3 The Flying Egg 83
   4 People Problems 85
   5 The Rescue 93
   6 Self-Organisation 95
   7 Team Problem-Solving 99
   8 Multi-Task Management 102

Appendix 2 Answers to Exercises 108

Glossary 110

Further Reading 112

Index 114

Acknowledgements

Firstly, I would like to thank both my mother and my better half, Edith, for their support and encouragement in seeing this book through to its conclusion.

Secondly, my sincere thanks to Brian Goodwin for his help and contribution to the exercises contained in this book. Brian is a training consultant with many years' experience in teambuilding.

Next my thanks go to all those managers whom I have known and whose efforts, both good and bad, to manage teams have unwittingly contributed to this book.

Last but by no means least, my special thanks to Nikki Read, whose editing skills, suggestions and help have been invaluable in compiling the finished book.

Preface

We normally associate the word 'team' with sport. However, in recent years many businesses and organisations have seen the benefits that can arise from working in teams and are keen to introduce the concept to their employees. Teams are particularly important for those companies and organisations employing Total Quality Control, Customer Care, Just-In-Time and similar systems.

Simply putting a group of individuals together in one place and expecting them to operate as a team is not the answer. Teams are like people, they need to be developed, nurtured and supported until they mature. Also, like people, teams will develop their own personalities.

The purpose of this book is to help you build and manage an effective, successful team. The principles involved are equally applicable to any type of team whether it be in an office, factory, retail outlet, hospital, educational establishment or in the field such as a sales force.

As training is such an important part of teambuilding, a selection of team exercises have been included in Appendix 1, designed for you to run as part of your team meetings or at training sessions.

Having read the book it will be up to you to put the good points into practice. Improvements will only happen if you help to make them happen.

John Humphries

1
Defining a Team

DEFINING GROUPS AND TEAMS

A **group** is a collection of individuals each with their own thoughts, ideas, abilities and objectives – the sort of gathering that you might encounter on a social occasion or indeed waiting at a bus stop.

A **team** is also a collection of individuals with their own thoughts, ideas and abilities but with a common objective and the willingness to share their ideas and to use their abilities to help their colleagues to achieve the objective. As mentioned in the Preface, we most readily associate a team with sport, but it is becoming increasingly used in the business world.

There are numerous definitions of the word 'team', but the following makes the concept clear:

A team is a group of people working together to achieve common objectives and willing to commit all their energies necessary to ensuring that the objectives are achieved.

RECOGNISING A SUCCESSFUL TEAM

Teams can be of any size from two people such as a tennis doubles team up to the fifty or more who comprise an American football squad.

Exploring the common factors needed for a successful team

Regardless of the size of the team or its objectives, successful teams will possess common factors:

- *Common objectives*. Each member will know what the objectives are and what they need to do to achieve them.

- *Commitment*. Everyone is totally committed to reaching the goals and is willing to forego any personal objectives which may cause conflict.

- *Communication.* The team members will talk to each other to exchange information, ask for and give help to their colleagues, encourage and motivate each other.

- *Confidence.* Members will be confident that everyone is a 'fully paid up' member of the team and can be relied upon to perform their tasks to the best of their ability.

- *Enjoyment.* It is noticeable that people involved in successful teams appear to be enjoying themselves.

- *Good leadership.* Every successful team will have a good leader who is recognised as such and accepted and respected by the team members.

- *Involvement.* Everyone is totally involved all the time with nobody hanging around wondering what to do.

- *Mutual trust.* It is vital that every member of the team trusts their colleagues. This is particularly important in terms of Health and Safety. If one person is at the top of a high ladder it is vital that they can trust their team mates to hold it steady and not wander off for a tea break.

- *Role identity.* Each member of the team will have a specific role to play. This ensures that no tasks are left undone.

- *Standards.* In addition to the objectives, each member of the team will know the standards expected of them in terms of both quality and behaviour.

- *Supportive.* Team members will help each other to reach the target. When one person has completed their particular job, they are willing to help others finish theirs.

- *Well trained.* Everyone is fully trained to perform their tasks to the highest standards and trained in working as a team.

BENEFITING FROM TEAMS

People working together as a team can:

- achieve goals more quickly and more efficiently than individuals working alone (see Appendix 1, Exercise 7)

- support and help each other to improve their skills

- become more confident and develop good interpersonal skills

- be more creative than individuals (see Appendix 1, Exercise 3)

- take risks that individuals may avoid

- be more flexible

- show commitment to the task and each other

- share information, knowledge and feelings (see Appendix 1, Exercise 1)

- be self-motivated

- enjoy their work by being with other people

- be easier to manage.

UNDERSTANDING DIFFERENT TYPES OF TEAMS

There are many different types of teams depending upon the tasks and objectives. Some require the team members to **work closely together** and be **reliant upon each other**, for example:

- project teams

- strategy teams

- departmental teams, e.g. personnel, administration, production

- operating theatre teams

- assembly teams

- football teams.

In other teams the members may **operate individually** but with **equal commitment** to achieving the objective. These could include:

- sales teams

- design teams

- maintenance teams

- data processing teams

- athletic teams.

A third type of team is one **comprising a number of smaller teams**. For example:

- a business company – the departments

- a military battalion – the platoons

- an orchestra – strings, woodwind, brass and percussion sections.

Before attempting to build a team, decide into which category it falls as this will help you to determine how you approach the task.

CASE STUDIES

Nigel leads a group

Nigel is a thrusting, successful young salesman who has recently been promoted to Regional Sales Manager. He is now responsible for six salespeople, several of whom are older and more experienced than him.

He believes that people should stand or fall on their own abilities and does not understand the reasons for or benefits of his group working as a team. As a result the salespeople rarely speak to each other and their main communication with Nigel is through the extensive weekly reports they have to complete and send to him. He will telephone them to criticise their efforts and occasionally arranges a meeting to tell them what has to be done.

The salespeople feel very isolated and certainly not part of a team.

Sue leads a team

Sue heads up her company's Human Resources Department. The department is responsible for the personnel and training functions. She has three personnel officers and two assistants, four trainers and a training administrator. She is an advocate of teamwork and currently her personnel staff work as one team and the trainers as another. Her aim is to get everyone working as one team.

She talks to everyone regularly on a face-to-face basis and organises regular meetings to exchange information and ideas. Her department is recognised as one of the most efficient in the company.

Tom has recently been given the task of forming teams

Tom is an ex-army physical training instructor and a qualified rugby union coach. He is the head physical education teacher at a large mixed school. Recently he has been asked to take responsibility for the coaching of the school's rugby teams. Although in the past he has been the member of several teams, he has never had to build and lead one and is having to learn as he goes. So far he has discovered a number of skilful individual players but is finding it difficult to blend them into a successful team.

SUMMARY

Groups	Teams
People work together.	People work for each other.
Information is given sparingly.	Information is shared openly.
Feelings are suppressed.	Feelings are expressed.
Conflict is accepted.	Conflict is worked through.
Trust is guarded.	Trust is shared.
People work for themselves.	People help each other.
Objectives may be unclear.	Objectives are always clear.
Failure is often blamed on others.	Success and failure are shared.
Goals may be personal.	Goals are common to all.
Leadership may not be apparent.	Good leadership prevails.

2
Leading the Team

Lead – 1. cause to go with one by guiding or showing the way 2. direct the actions or opinions of 3. guide by persuasion, example or argument.

Leader – a person followed by others.

(Oxford English Dictionary)

Leaders go under a variety of titles depending upon the circumstances: directors, managers, supervisors, captains, officers, team leaders and so on.

UNDERSTANDING HOW PEOPLE BECOME LEADERS

There are natural, born leaders and those who are put into leadership positions. Generally speaking, it is the latter group that constitute the majority of team leaders in business today.

People become leaders in one of four ways:

1. **By appointment**. Such people are normally promoted or elected to lead a group of people to achieve certain objectives. Unfortunately, too often the reason behind the appointment is that the person was good at doing their original job, e.g. a good salesperson, an excellent accountant, an international footballer, etc. They may not possess either the qualities or the desire to lead and rarely obtain the necessary training.

2. **By experience or knowledge**. This is often known as situational leadership. The person becomes the leader because of their knowledge or experience of a particular situation. For example, those chosen to lead an expedition or a company takeover will have the required experience. Such people also become leaders in emergencies. A medically trained person will usually take control at the scene of an accident.

3. **By personality**. These people are rare and often reluctant leaders. However, they possess certain qualities that influence other people to follow them. Famous (or notorious) leaders such as Mahatma Ghandi, Nelson Mandela and Adolf Hitler fall into this category.

4. **By birthright**. Less common than in the past, there are nevertheless people who are born into a leadership role. These may include people born to wealthy parents and who will inherit large tracts of land together with those who work on the estate; or the son or daughter of the owner of a business who automatically takes over when the owner retires. This does not necessarily make them good leaders but they are leaders all the same.

DEFINING LEADERSHIP QUALITIES

Can anyone become a leader? Some of the necessary qualities have to be inborn, part of your personality, others can be learned. So what are these qualities?

Select **ten** of the following qualities that you believe are essential for good leadership:

Commitment   Integrity   Flexible
          Supportive   Reliable
Trustworthy   Awareness   Creative
          Fair minded   Good communicator
Decisive   Empathy   Stable
          Stress free   Foresight
Tough minded   Common sense   Intelligent
          Open minded   Planner

Although the following list is not in order of importance, unless you have the first quality, good leadership will be very difficult.

* **Good communication skills**. This does not only mean being able to give orders but covers the whole area of oral communication including listening (see Chapter 5).

* **Commitment**. It is essential to demonstrate your commitment to achieving the objectives of the team and your commitment to each team member.

- **Empathy**. Being able to see other points of view without necessarily agreeing or disagreeing with them.

- **Integrity**. A leader must be seen to be honest in dealing with people and situations.

- **Trustworthy**. You need to show your team that they can trust you to keep your word and maintain confidences.

- **Reliable**. When you make a promise, keep it.

- **Decisive**. When you are called upon to make a decision, make one. Prevarication is not only time wasting but can lose you credibility.

- **Open minded**. Be prepared to listen and give due consideration to ideas and suggestions from the team.

- **Planner**. Being able to identify the strengths of the team and use them in planning to achieve the objectives.

- **Awareness**. Being fully aware of what is happening all around you especially changes which might affect the team and the objectives.

- **Supportive**. Being able to give help and guidance to the team as and when required and also to protect individuals when necessary.

- **Stable**. Emotional stability is essential so that everyone knows where they stand with you. Your feelings, particularly negative ones, should be carefully controlled.

- **Common sense**. To be used in all circumstances, especially when dealing with people.

- **Fair minded**. Treat everyone equally. You must be able to control any prejudices or biases you may have about people and things.

- **Tough minded**. You should not be afraid to be 'tough' on people when the occasion demands, but it should be kept for emergencies not to disguise your personal failings.

- **Creative**. Thinking laterally and being prepared to experiment with new ideas and methods.

- **Flexible**. As a good leader you should be able to change your approach and style to best suit the situation.

- **Stress free**. Although this is difficult in the modern world, a leader who is stressed tends to drive, not lead.

- **Foresight**. You need to be able to look ahead and foresee possible problems before they happen.

- **Intelligent**. You should be able to vary your behaviour in response to different situations and requirements in a sensible and intelligent manner.

Earning respect

To be an effective leader, you need the respect of your team. Contrary to the belief of many managers, respect does not come with the job title, it has to be earned. This can be achieved by demonstrating most if not all of the qualities listed above and by acknowledging that the team works **with** you and not for you. Give credit where it is due and constructive criticism when necessary.

ASSESSING THE ROLES AND RESPONSIBILITIES OF A LEADER

Roles and responsibilities will, of course, vary depending upon the level of responsibility given to the leader.

The captain of a cricket team has the responsibility for strategic decisions such as whether or not to bat on winning the toss, when to declare an innings, where to place his fielders, which bowlers to use and when. As a result, the success or failure of the team is largely dependent on these decisions.

On the other hand, the captain of a football team has a less influential role, only being able to lead by example and encourage and cajole those players within earshot.

The role of the leader of a work-based team will depend on their level in the company's hierarchy. It is likely that they will be responsible for all the functions of the sports captain together with a few more.

Exploring responsibilities

Typical responsibilities of a leader include:

- **Executive**. Determines the objectives, sets the standards and directs the team to achieving them.

- **Planner**. Decides how the team should reach its goals.

- **Controller**. Decides how the team should be organised, using the skills and abilities of each member to the best advantage to the team.

- **Communicator**. Gives direction and information, seeks information and listens to the team.

- **Exemplar**. Serves as a model of behaviour for the team and leads by example.

- **Motivator**. Maintains the morale of the team by knowing the needs of each individual and satisfying them to the best of his or her ability.

- **Delegator**. Gives appropriate tasks, duties and responsibilities to team members to suit their strengths.

- **Involver**. Encourages the team to become involved in all aspects of the team's activities: decision-making, problem-solving, making suggestions, etc.

- **Supporter**. Provides help and support to individuals as necessary.

- **Coach**. Develops the skills of team members.

- **Resource manager**. Uses all the resources available to enable the goals to be achieved.

- **Recruiter**. Selects the most suitable people to join the team.

- **Visionary**. Has vision of the future and conveys this to the team.

- **Figurehead**. Provides a focus for team unity and identification.

- **Representative**. Represents the team to other teams and individuals.

Outlining the demands

There are three main demands on every leader:

1. *Task needs* – to get the job done.

2 *Group needs* – to build and maintain team spirit.

3. *Individual needs* – to satisfy the needs of the individual within the needs of the task and the group.

How successful a leader is in meeting these demands will largely depend on the style of leadership they employ.

LOOKING AT DIFFERENT LEADERSHIP STYLES

Styles of leadership can be categorised in a number of ways. The style used by the inexperienced, untrained leader will be the one they feel most comfortable with although it may not be the most appropriate or effective for the situation. The style adopted will often be the one by which they have been led in the past.

The way in which someone approaches leadership will be influenced by their preference for either the task or the people.

Task-oriented preference

'The most important thing is to get the job done on time and within the budget. If we don't achieve the target then we are all out of a job. I don't have time to worry about the concerns of the people. If they don't like the way things are, they can leave.'

In today's business world, this is the approach taken by too many managers largely because they are put under excessive pressure by their bosses. The objectives may well be achieved but the result is a demotivated, discontented workforce, many of whom may well leave as a result.

Does this style have a place? Yes, in an emergency; for example, when it is essential to evacuate a burning building. Occasionally it can be used to meet a short-term objective where failure may jeopardise the future existence of a company.

People-oriented preference

'We should try to reach the objective but as long as my people are happy it doesn't matter too much. The most important thing is to have a contented workforce. I don't want any conflicts or hassles.'

This may sound ideal, but most people need some sort of target or deadline to give them impetus and any leader who takes this approach will quickly lose control and credibility.

Is there a case for this style? If people have been working under pressure to reach a goal, once it has been achieved there is no harm in a short period of relaxation to reward the team. The caring professions will tend to be more people- than task-oriented simply because their business is people.

- The good leader will strike a balance between task and people.

Dictate or abdicate?

There are three universally recognised styles of leadership. Which do you favour? All will be revealed once you have completed the following simple questionnaire.

Read each statement carefully and tick it if you agree with it.

1. Teams should be left to make their own decisions. ☐

2. The leader should always give detailed instructions. ☐

3. Suggestions for improvement should be encouraged. ☐

4. Regular training is important. ☐

5. As the leader you should delegate as much as possible. ☐

6. Targets should always be set by the leaders. ☐

7. It is better to let conflicts resolve themselves. ☐

8. The leader should share decision-making with the team. ☐

9. The team should be closely supervised. ☐

10. All decisions should be carefully explained to the team. ☐

11. The team should be responsible for solving its problems. ☐

12. The leader should set the standards expected from the team. ☐

13. The leader should develop the team's skills through coaching. ☐

14. Team members should be self-motivated. ☐

15. A leader should strictly control the activities of the team. ☐

16. The leader should act as the guide and mentor to the team. ☐

17. There is no need for the leader to become involved in the day-to-day routines of the team. ☐

18. The leader is totally responsible for the team's actions. ☐

Scoring

For each tick you have placed, circle the appropriate number on the table below, then add up the number of circles in each column. The highest total will indicate your preferred style.

Directing	Supporting	Delegating
2	3	1
6	4	5
9	8	7
12	10	11
15	13	14
18	16	17
_____	_____	_____

There is no totally wrong style, it all depends when they are used.

Directing

The leader gives precise instructions and closely supervises the team. There is little room for creativity or initiative from the team. Leaders who constantly operate in this style are often seen as exercising their authority in a dictatorial manner and consider that the team work *for* them rather than *with* them. There is a tendency to accept all the kudos when the team are successful but blame the team for any failures. Such leaders are usually task-oriented and may use fear tactics to drive the team.

This style may be appropriate when a decision has to be made quickly and the consequences are high. It can also be used with someone who has little experience of the company's policies, priorities or methods.

Supporting

The leader supports the team's efforts towards accomplishing the goals, with help, guidance and coaching. The responsibility for solving problems and making decisions is shared with the team. Successes and failures are also shared. The leader using this style will praise the team members for their efforts as well as their results but will not hesitate to take corrective action when necessary.

Most people respond well to this style of leadership, especially if they have some experience of the task and the company.

Delegating

The leader hands over the responsibilities for decision-making and problem-solving to the team. There is a tendency to let people get on with it and intervene as little as possible. If this style is taken to extremes, the leader may be seen as abdicating their role.

This style may be appropriate with very experienced team members in whom the leader has total trust and confidence.

- Once again, the good leader will apply a combination of these styles to suit the people involved.

UNDERSTANDING SITUATIONAL LEADERSHIP

The leader of any group of people will face a variety of situations for which different leadership styles are available. Robert Tannenbaum and Warren Schmidt have identified six styles which depend upon the relative influence of the leader and the team (see Figure 1).

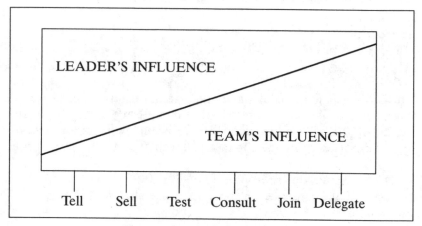

Fig. 1.   The six leadership styles.

- **Tell**. The leader simply tells the team what to do and the team has no say in the matter.

- **Sell**. Similar to Tell, but this time the leader gives reasons or benefits for the action to be taken.

- **Test**. In this case the leader puts forward his/her solution or decision and asks for the team's agreement.

- **Consult**. The leader explains the situation to the team, suggests a solution and asks the team for their solutions.

- **Join**. As with Consult, the leader explains the situation but then joins the team to explore and discuss possible solutions.

- **Delegate**. Once again the leader explains the situation and asks the team to come up with some solutions, but this time the leader takes no part in the discussion and agrees to accept the team's conclusions.

Exercising flexibility

Although most people will have their preferred leadership style, the good leader should exercise flexibility and use the right style for each situation as it occurs.

IDENTIFYING INFLUENCES ON LEADERSHIP STYLE

There are three factors which can influence the style used: the leader's personality, the team, the situation.

- **The leader's personality**

  - how strongly the leader feels they must exercise their authority

  - how secure the leader feels in certain situations

  - the leader's previous experience of leadership

  - how much the leader trusts the team

  - how committed the leader is to the objectives.

- **The team**

  - the team's knowledge and experience

  - how ready the team is to accept responsibility

  - how prepared the team members are to support each other

  - the team's commitment to the objectives

  - whether the team prefers to be directed or guided.

- **The situation**

  - the type of organisation; autocratic or democratic

  - time constraints; time pressure may not be conducive for consultation

  - only the leader may have experience of the situation

  - the seriousness of the consequence of failure

  - the degree to which the situation will affect the team.

CASE STUDIES

Nigel adopts a task-oriented style of leadership

Nigel has been told by his Sales Director that sales revenue has to increase by 15 per cent. He calls a meeting with his team and tells them that they have to increase the sales revenue by 20 per cent and the only way to do this is by increasing their call rate, reducing discounts and having a more aggressive approach. Nigel tells his salespeople that he expects to see a significant improvement in orders and revenue by the end of the quarter. Anyone who fails could be looking for another job.

As a result, a very demotivated group of people leave the meeting. There has been no opportunity to discuss problems such as the company's pricing strategy and competitive activity. Their feelings towards Nigel are negative to say the least.

Sue adopts a people-oriented style of leadership

Sue has been asked to consider the possibility of producing a company newsletter on a quarterly basis. She sends a memo to each of her team outlining the proposal and asking them to think about the feasibility of the project, possible contents and suggestions for a title, ready for a meeting the following week. Having been involved in a similar project with her previous company, Sue has plenty of ideas.

The meeting is run as a 'brainstorm' session and is very lively. Everyone has ample opportunity to contribute and Sue feeds in her suggestions along with everyone else. As a result, everyone is very enthusiastic about the idea and one of the trainers agrees to draw up a feasibility report for the directors.

Tom tries to appease the people while doubting whether the task will be achieved

Tom is beginning to panic. The first inter-school rugby match is less than a week away and he still does not know which players will make the team. There are plenty of skilful forwards but few backs. Eventually he selects what he considers to be the fifteen best players and two substitutes although he knows that the team will be unbalanced and some of the players are out of position.

Although the team scores two tries and a penalty, they concede three tries, two penalties and a drop goal and so lose the match. After the match the forwards blame the backs especially the scrum half and team spirit is at zero. Tom realises that he will have to make a lot of improvements before the next match.

SUMMARY

Good leadership means:

- being aware of the needs of the task, group and individuals
- changing your style to suit the situation
- knowing the strengths and weaknesses of your team
- encouraging the team to become involved where appropriate
- having good communication skills
- gaining the commitment of the team to achieve the goals
- being supportive
- sharing successes
- encouraging and listening to ideas and suggestions from the team
- ensuring that everyone knows what is expected of them
- engendering a positive team spirit
- being part of the team as well as the leader
- accepting your responsibilities
- earning the respect of the team by your example.

EXERCISES

1. What leadership styles have been used in the above case studies? What would be the most appropriate? (For suggested answers, see Appendix 2.)

2. Give examples of appropriate situations for each of Tannenbaum and Schmidt's leadership styles.

3. Analyse the preferred leadership styles of your colleagues.

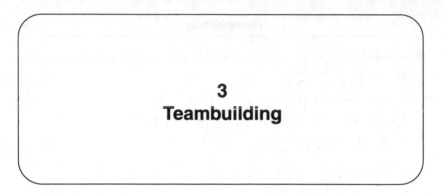

3
Teambuilding

QUESTIONS BEFORE YOU BEGIN

As a manager you may be in the fortunate position of being able to build your team from scratch. It is more likely, however, that you have inherited a group of people who may or may not be working as a team. Whichever the case, before attempting to build a team, there are four questions that must be answered:

- What are the objectives?
- What needs to be done to achieve them?
- What resources do I need?
- Do I need a team?

What are the objectives?
These will, of course, depend upon the purpose of your team and the demands of senior management. Typical objectives include:

- increase revenue
- reduce costs
- produce products
- provide information
- create ideas
- improve safety
- tend patients.

Whatever the objectives, they must be more defined than those listed above; for example:

- Increase revenue (or reduce costs) by what percentage within what timescale?

- Produce how many products by when?

- Provide what information, for whom, by when?

- Create ideas for what purpose?

- Improve safety to what standard?

- Tend patients to achieve what?

Objectives must also be achievable otherwise people immediately become demotivated and look for excuses for failure. They must also be measurable.

It is your responsibility to clarify your team's objectives and ensure that they can be met.

What needs to be done?

Having agreed the goals, you need to sit down and work out exactly what needs to be done in order to reach them.

Prepare a plan, listing what has to be done together with target deadlines, what resources you need and what skills are required.

What resources do I need?

Managers have a number of resources at their disposal:

- people

- equipment

- finance

- space

- time

- information.

Although it is essential that sufficient equipment, finance, time, etc. is available, we will concentrate on **people** as it is they who will form the team and make it successful or not.

People are very different from any of the other resources. One £1,000 is very much like any other £1,000 and barring any dramatic moves in the money market will have the same value on Monday, Tuesday, Wednesday and so on. Regardless of their design, the function of chairs remains the same throughout their lives. However, with the possible exception of identical twins, no two people will have exactly the same characteristics, personalities, attitudes and needs. To complicate matters even further, these can change on a regular basis depending upon their health, their feelings towards other people and how they believe they are valued. The main difference between human beings and other resources is that the former have emotions and feelings.

Some people are natural 'team members' and enjoy working in co-operation with others, while other people prefer to work alone and find it difficult to operate in close liaison with their colleagues.

People will bring different skills, abilities, knowledge, personalities and attitudes to the team. It is your job to make sure that your team have the right skills, knowledge, etc. to achieve the targets.

Do I need a team?

This may seem a strange question to ask in a book about teams. However, the fact is that not every 'work group' needs to become a team in order to be successful. If the group consists of people with specialist skills each performing specific tasks, they may not need to be moulded into a team to achieve their goals. For example, with a 'team' of salespeople who each sell a different range of products to a different market, there would be little value in spending time and effort making them into a team in the true sense of the word.

Teams are only needed when:

* you are experiencing rapid changes

* you are dealing with a problem where nobody knows the answer

* there is uncertainty about the task and a need to share the problem with others

* there is a real need for people to work closely together.

If you do not fulfil any of these criteria, then you don't need a team.

IDENTIFYING STRENGTHS AND WEAKNESSES

One of your first tasks when trying to convert your group into a team is to discover the strengths and weaknesses of each individual. For the purpose of this exercise we must assume that any weaknesses in their ability to do their jobs are dealt with separately by the appropriate training and coaching. We are concerned with strengths and weaknesses relating to working as a team.

You can do this in several ways:

By observation
Carefully watch each person at work. How well do they interact with their colleagues? Do they help each other? Do they talk to one another? Do they cause any conflicts? Do they take lunch breaks together? Do they share personal confidences?

By interviewing each one individually
Explain that the purpose of the interview is to engender a team spirit and tell them the benefits of working as a team.

From your observations, praise them for the positives and question them about the negatives. Your aim is to discover the causes for any negative behaviours. It is important to approach this matter in a non-critical way.

For example
You may have identified that the person you are talking to has shown a particular antipathy towards another member of your staff. You may say, 'I notice that you rarely have anything to do with Ted. What's the reason for that? Then keep quiet and wait for an answer. Hopefully the reason is something that can be resolved between the three of you.

By testing
There are numerous psychometric tests available which are designed to identify personality traits. The results will indicate whether or not the individual is a 'team player'. If you intend to use such methods, they must be introduced very carefully as most people are suspicious of these tests. In addition, despite the in-built checks, there is no guarantee that people will answer them honestly and many will try to beat the system.

Most of these tests have to be administered by a qualified person and therefore can be quite expensive.

If you are interested in pursuing this matter further, I suggest that you talk to your company's Human Resources department first.

To help you with the observation and interviewing, you may wish to use the simple questionnaire in Figure 2.

Name	Yes	No
Do they interact well with colleagues?		
Do they offer help to others?		
Do they talk regularly to colleagues?		
Do they put forward ideas to aid the team?		
Do they participate in meetings?		
Do they help to solve problems?		
Do they respond well when offered help?		
Do they enjoy working in a team?		
Do they socialise with their colleagues?		
Do they ever cause interpersonal conflicts?		
Do they complain about other people?		
Do they moan when things are not going well?		
Can they be developed into good team members?		

Fig. 2. Questionnaire to help with observation and interviewing.

IDENTIFYING TEAM ROLES

Each member of a team will have two roles:

1. their specialist or technical role – this is the job that they perform, be it selling, driving, designing, accounting, data collection or whatever
2. their team role – as the team develops, each individual will assume a specific role within the team.

Considerable research has been done to identify these roles, which can be classified as follows:

- **The natural leader**. Some people have a natural ability to take charge. They are concerned with teamwork and have the ability to clarify the aims and organise the team to achieve them. Although extrovert by nature they exercise their authority in a relaxed, non-aggressive manner.

- **The activator**. These people are only concerned with getting things done. They tend to be impulsive, impatient, competitive, domineering and often intolerant of those who prefer to think and plan first. Although they undoubtedly make things happen, they can often upset other team members.

- **The thinker**. Such people are usually full of creative ideas and often make suggestions for doing things differently and are quick to criticise others. They require acknowledgement and praise for their ideas and can be useful members if handled properly. They have a tendency to withdraw into themselves if their suggestions are not accepted.

- **The organiser**. These people are good at turning ideas and decisions into workable plans. They like a defined and disciplined approach and enjoy making schedules and charts. Whilst being efficient and methodical, they can also be negative and slow to adapt to rapidly changing situations.

- **The checker**. This individual is obsessed with meeting deadlines and constantly keeps an eye on the time. They need to check every detail and can get bogged down in the minutiae. Such people keep the team aware of the need for urgency and attention to detail.

- **The judge**. The most objective and uninvolved member of the team, this person provides dispassionate analysis and likes time to consider. They are calm and dependable but can appear tactless and disparaging which can affect team morale.

- **The supporter**. These are the real team players and are concerned with encouraging team spirit and unity. They build on other people's ideas and offer help and support to others. Supporters dislike confrontation and will try to avoid or defuse it.

The team role that an individual takes on is largely dependent upon their personality and is thus difficult to change. As each of the above has their advantages, ideally one would look for a mix and as the team leader you would need to develop their positives and reduce their negatives.

In an ideal world a team would consist of one from each category and several supporters.

- Into which category would you place each individual in your team? Is the mix the right one for you? Trying some of the exercises in Appendix 1 will help you identify your team members' team roles.

ALLOCATING ROLES

Team members need to know the part they are expected to play within the team. The mix of skills and roles must be sufficient to undertake the tasks in hand. Although roles may overlap, they must not conflict.

If the required roles are not filled naturally, it is your responsibility to fill the gaps by allocating roles to people and training them where necessary. Flexibility is the key word. Everyone should be capable of taking on two or more skills and roles when necessary to cover for absenteeism. This includes your role as leader.

A good example of a group of specialists working together as a highly efficient team can be seen in the pit crews of a Formula One racing team. By constantly practising together, when a car arrives at the pits during a race, the most efficient teams can change all four wheels and fill the tanks with fuel in 8 to 10 seconds.

BUILDING THE TEAM

It is generally recognised that teams go through four stages in the building process:

1. forming

2 storming

3 norming

4 performing.

Forming
This is where people tend to:

- be polite to one another

- be guarded in what they say or do

- test each other out

- say a lot or very little.

As the leader, this is your opportunity to:

- talk to individuals, determine their strengths, weaknesses, experience and what they hope to achieve
- clarify the team's purpose and goals
- introduce simple teambuilding exercises.

Storming
Now people may:

- test your leadership abilities
- express opinions about their colleagues and/or work methods
- become demotivated.

This can be a difficult stage and it will be helpful if you:

- invite questions and opinions
- are proactive rather than reactive
- watch for signs of conflict and deal with them immediately
- arrange a meeting to discuss any problems that you perceive.

Norming
- The team is now beginning to gel.
- Standards and ground rules are emerging, particularly in respect of behaviours.

This can be a tricky stage for any leader as the group could slip back to the previous stage. To help prevent this you should:

- listen and watch what is happening in the team
- reinforce the team's purpose and goals
- maintain good communications with the team
- keep an open mind and seek out new ideas.

Performing
Once the team has reached this stage you will see that:

- individuals help and support each other
- information and ideas are shared
- problems are solved and decisions made
- everyone is willing to 'muck in'
- there is increased tolerance and flexibility
- energy is expended in the right direction
- more humour and enjoyment emerges.

However, this is not the time for you to sit back and relax as:

- individuals may leave and join the team
- external influences may affect the team and its targets.

It is your responsibility as the leader to manage any changes that may occur and continue to encourage team work.

CASE STUDIES

Nigel does not believe in teambuilding

Nigel has assumed the role of leader along with his title of Regional Sales Manager. As he has no time for team work, his staff confine themselves to their specialist roles, i.e. selling. They are expected to solve their own problems and any ideas or suggestions that they make are quickly dismissed. However, it is not unknown for Nigel to take a suggestion, develop it and put it forward as his own idea.

The team are not encouraged to contact or help each other. Nigel's idea of support is to tell his people to work harder.

Sue advocates teambuilding

Recently one of Sue's personnel officers left. When she is recruiting a replacement, Sue looks for someone who not only has the necessary skills and experience to perform the job but also possesses the right personality and attitude to fit in with the existing team.

This means that when the new person arrives, they are quickly accepted by their new colleagues and Sue's job is much easier as there is no disruption to the team.

Tom is trying to build a team

Tom has identified one of his players as having natural leadership qualities. Although not the most skilful player, this young man is able to exercise authority in a quiet, yet forceful manner and appears to have the respect of his team mates. Tom has therefore decided to appoint him as captain.

SUMMARY

- Clarify the objectives of the team.
- Analyse what has to be done to achieve them.
- Decide what resources are needed.
- Identify the strengths and weaknesses of the group.
- Buy in missing skills if possible or train the existing people.
- Allocate team roles where necessary.
- Ensure that the team members are flexible and willing to take on additional tasks when required.

4
Teamworking

Teamworking is very different from teambuilding. While teambuilding is about gathering together the right skills, experience, characteristics and attitudes, teamworking is about getting that group of people to actually operate together as a team.

Teamworking can best be described as:

Everyone – having a common set of objectives

– knowing what has to be done

– pulling in the same direction

– pulling their weight

– helping others when necessary

– supporting each other

– joining in to retrieve a potential disaster

– sharing success and failure

– enjoying working with everyone else

– moving forward together.

Nobody – feeling left out

– complaining in times of crisis

– causing conflict within the team

– putting their own ambitions first

– blaming others for failure.

UNDERSTANDING THE BENEFITS OF TEAMWORK

Whenever I visit a company, it is easy to identify those departments working as a team and those remaining a group of employees. The team has a positive buzz about it and everyone appears to be busy and enjoy working together. Smiles and laughter are good indicators of teamwork.

Talking to managers of successful teams reveals such things as a high degree of self-motivation, good timekeeping, low absenteeism, regular achievement of goals and above all, being easy to manage.

To summarise the benefits of teamworking:

- Goals more easily and efficiently reached.
- A positive attitude from everyone.
- More creativity and innovation.
- Fewer errors.
- Crises and problems identified and dealt with quickly.
- Individuals motivated by being part of the team.
- High degree of self-development.
- Allows a 'hands off' management style.

CREATING THE RIGHT ENVIRONMENT

The big question that most managers ask at this point is 'How do we get the team to work together?' The answer is: simply by creating the right environment, one that will appeal to the team and make them want to be successful. This can be done by:

- clarifying the objectives
- sharing information
- leading by example
- motivating
- involving the team in decision-making and problem-solving
- welcoming ideas and creativity
- training
- encouraging the team to perform well

- making meetings worthwhile

- offering opportunities to 'bond'.

CLARIFYING THE OBJECTIVES

It is essential that every member of the team knows and understands the objectives. In addition to telling the team what these objectives are, write or print them in bold letters on a piece of paper and position it where it can be constantly seen.

If there are any changes to the goals, however small, make sure that these are communicated to the team and update the notice.

SHARING INFORMATION

You will receive various quantities and qualities of information. The only information that you should keep to yourself is that which is highly confidential. Share all other data with your team, even that which does not directly affect their work. For instance, changes in personnel, achievements by other people in the organisation, new developments and so on. (see Appendix 1, Exercise 1 on sharing information.)

LEADING BY EXAMPLE

This does not mean that you have to be the best at doing all the jobs in the team. Simply act as you would want the team to act, show commitment, dress appropriately, communicate openly, maintain good timekeeping, be positive and be prepared to 'muck in' when necessary.

MOTIVATING

Despite what many management pundits claim, you cannot motivate a team, only the individuals in it.

Everybody has one or more needs and it is the prospect of satisfying these needs that motivates them. 'Needs' differ from 'wants' in that the former are essential and the later desirable.

As a manager, you have to realise that people have different needs and it is your responsibility to identify them and help the individuals to satisfy them. Whilst it may not be within your authority to satisfy needs such as money or promotion, there are many that you can satisfy.

Most people have one or more of the following needs:

- **Responsibility**. The need to have something for which they are responsible and accountable. You can deal with this through good delegation.

- **Respect**. Simply needing other people to respect the fact that they are individuals with ideas and opinions. Getting such people involved in making decisions and solving problems and asking for their suggestions can be sufficient.

- **Reward**. Not necessarily money or prizes, but sincere and genuine praise for a job well done can usually satisfy this need. Don't forget to praise effort as well as results.

- **Recognition**. People need to be recognised by others for who they are and that they actually exist. Make sure that you acknowledge and communicate with them on a regular basis.

As has already been mentioned, members of successful teams will be self-motivated to achieve good results both to satisfy their self-esteem and for the sake of their colleagues. This does not mean that you can relinquish your responsibility in this matter.

INVOLVING

It is important to involve the team in making decisions and solving problems, particularly those that affect the team. You can ask individuals whether they have experience of the matter, or the whole team. In which case adopt the Consult or Join styles of leadership.

If the team seems reluctant to come forward with suggestions, you may wish to use one or other of the following techniques.

Brainstorming

Gather the team together, explain the problem clearly together with the objective and ask them to shout out their ideas. Each suggestion is written on a flip chart for all to see. Ask one of your team to be the scribe while you sit with your team – this helps to make it less formal.

To be successful, apply these rules:

- Every suggestion, however ludicrous it may seem, is written up.

- Ideas are written randomly on the sheet, not in the form of a list.

- No judgements or criticisms are made at this stage.

- Continue until the suggestions dry up.

Each idea is then briefly discussed and either discarded or put forward for further consideration. This method is very suitable when creative ideas are sought.

Brain writing
For this the team should sit round a table with a sheet of paper in front of them. The problem is explained and they are then asked to write down a possible solution. After two or three minutes, the papers are passed to the left and the team then have to build upon the suggestion in front of them. After a few more minutes the papers are once again passed to the left and the solutions added to. Continue this three or four times. At the end you should have a number of solutions that have been thought through by the team. These are then read out and the team can decide which one to adopt. This technique can be used when the problem is more technical or serious, such as improving the workflow.

WELCOMING IDEAS

You must demonstrate that you welcome ideas from your team by being prepared to listen and consider each one. When you believe a suggestion is practicable, either ask the person to develop it further, or put it to the team for their input. If it is not practicable, then carefully explain the reasons why. Always thank people for their ideas whatever the outcome.

TRAINING

Team training is dealt with in Chapter 7. However, it is also your responsibility to ensure that everyone is adequately trained to perform their tasks, either by on-job training, or by sending them on a course.

It is also important that you give individuals the opportunity for development training in such areas as supervisory/management skills, marketing techniques, finance or whatever is appropriate to aid their future prospects.

ENCOURAGING THE TEAM TO PERFORM WELL

You may wish to offer the team a small incentive, such as a bottle of wine each, store vouchers or whatever your budget will allow, for reaching the team target. This should have the effect of promoting co-operation among the team.

I would not recommend offering individual incentives as this can lead to internal competition and will result in people having their own agenda causing splits within the team which is exactly what you don't want.

Do not forget to give praise for effort as well as results.

MAKING MEETINGS WORTHWHILE

Too many meetings are considered to be a waste of time. This is because they were either not necessary in the first place or poorly managed or controlled.

You will need to have the occasional meeting as part of the team-working process. Here are a few tips to help make them worthwhile to everyone involved.

- Only have a meeting when it is really necessary.

- Prepare an agenda, however simple. It should contain:

  – the date and venue

  – the start and finish times

  – the topics to be discussed.

- Distribute the agenda at least 24 hours before the meeting.

- Start on time.

- Stick to the topics listed.

- Control the meeting by inviting everyone to contribute by name – bring in.

- Stop people hogging the meeting by thanking them and immediately either inviting someone else to speak or by summarising.

- Summarise the points agreed.

- Agree action plans.

- Conclude the meeting on time. Use natural breaks such as lunch as a finishing time.

Ask members of your team to chair meetings as this will both involve them and aid their personal development.

OFFERING OPPORTUNITIES TO BOND

Bonding is one of the 'in things' at present, but I would not suggest that your team spend time hugging one another or indulge in in-depth analyses of each others' personalities. Activities such as paintball, go-karting or even a team dinner with partners can help them relate to each other outside the work place. You could actually use such activities as incentives to the team.

CASE STUDIES

Nigel holds a meeting

On Friday evening, Nigel phones each of his salespeople and tells them to report to the office at 9.00am the following Monday for a meeting. When several of them protest that they have appointments for the Monday, he simply tells them to rearrange them. (Remember, it is Friday evening.)

Everyone duly assembles on time and are told to go the conference room. When they are seated, Nigel immediately launches into a tirade of criticism about their performance over the past six months. This is despite the fact that three of the group have already reached their sales targets. If anyone attempts to say something they are overruled by Nigel.

He concludes by telling them that they have one month to improve or they can look for another job. He gives them no suggestion or help but leaves it to them.

At the end of the meeting, one of the salesmen, who has achieved his target, goes up to Nigel, tells him what he thinks of him, hands in his notice and says that he is going to see the Sales Director. So not only has Nigel lost his best salesman, he is also likely to have an unpleasant meeting with his director.

Sue gets her team involved

Sue has decided that it is time that the company's induction programme be revised and updated. She explains the problem to her team and invites them to a meeting in three days time.

Sue decides to run the meeting as a brainstorm session. One of the assistant personnel officers writes each suggestion on a flip chart. When the ideas have dried up, each is discussed and either discarded or accepted by the team.

Sue then asks two of the trainers and one personnel officer to put together an induction programme using the suggestions agreed and they will all meet again in two weeks time to finalise it.

The result is a new and exciting induction programme to which everyone is committed.

Tom provides an incentive for the team

Although Tom wants to improve the skills of each player, he also wants them to play for each other as a team. He decides to award 'colours', in the form of a scarf, to each player when they have appeared in three winning teams.

To further encourage team spirit, he arranges with a local supplier to provide small cloth badges each time the team wins. The badge contains the name of the opponents and the score and can be sewn onto the scarf.

This proves to be very popular and has the desired results, so much so that Tom instigates a similar system for the 2nd XV.

SUMMARY

- Having built your team, it is essential that they continue to work together as a team.

- It is your responsibility as the team leader to create the right atmosphere.

- By motivating the individuals, you will motivate the team.

- Keep the team involved in making decisions which affect them.

- Encourage ideas from the team.

- Regular team training will help to keep them together.

- Make team meetings interesting and worthwhile.

- Where practical, use social activities to bond your team.

5
Communicating with your Team

Good communication is perhaps the most important ingredient in helping a team to work well together. Each member must feel free to talk openly to the other members, including the leader, in the knowledge that they will be listened to; and likewise, they must be prepared to listen to others.

It is often said that the one thing that distinguishes the human race from the rest of the animal kingdom is our ability to communicate with one another through a highly developed, sophisticated system of language. That being the case, it is our responsibility to ensure that we use this gift to everyone's benefit.

As this book is about working in teams, we will confine ourselves to oral communications for it is hoped that it is rarely if every necessary to write to each other.

IDENTIFYING THE PURPOSES OF COMMUNICATION

We learn to communicate from an early age, but why? The main purposes of communication are:

- to give information
- to seek information
- to give our ideas and opinions
- to discover other people's ideas and opinions
- to express our feelings and emotions
- to get action
- to change attitudes and behaviours
- to be accepted by others.

We all use these reasons at one time or another and when operating as a team it is important to recognise and accept your colleagues' reasons even though they may not always appear to be appropriate.

ANALYSING THE CAUSES OF COMMUNICATION BREAKDOWNS

On the surface, communication may seem very simple. After all we do it all the time. However, there are numerous barriers or filters which mean that people do not always receive the same message that we are sending. These can be divided into **physical** and **emotional** barriers.

Physical barriers
These would include:

- noise such as traffic, other people talking, etc.

- interruptions by the telephone, people and so on

- environment: too hot, too cold, too dark, too bright

- unfamiliar accents and dialects

- hearing and speech impairments

- using jargon inappropriately

- timing: trying to talk to someone when they are about to do something.

Emotional barriers
Again unlike other animals, we have strong feelings and emotions which may not be known to the person we are talking with. These emotions can also cause barriers, for example:

- prejudice about the other person, their age, gender, appearance

- experience of talking with this person in the past may have been unpleasant

- status – the other person's position in relation to ours may be a barrier

- making assumptions and jumping to conclusions – 'We've heard it all before'

- personality – are you passive, submissive, aggressive or assertive (see further, below)?

It is important to recognise that these barriers exist and it is your responsibility to reduce or eliminate them in order to ensure that your communication is as effective as possible.

See Appendix 1, Exercise 1, for an example of how to stimulate discussion about communication issues in your team.

IDENTIFYING COMMUNICATION BEHAVIOURS

When we talk to one another, particularly in groups or teams, we use certain communication 'behaviours'. Some of these are positive and help us to communicate effectively, while others are negative and produce barriers to good communication.

The following is a list of positive and negative behaviours, most of them with an example of how they can be expressed verbally.

Positive behaviours

- **Proposing.**   Putting forward new ideas, suggestions or courses of action.
  'Let's all go to lunch together.'

- **Building**   Adding to or developing a proposal made by someone else.
  'That's a good idea and then we can discuss what to do this afternoon.'

- **Giving.**   Giving information or opinions to others.
  'We've only got ten minutes left.'

- **Seeking.**   Asking for information or opinions from other people.
  'What time is it?' 'What do you think of that idea?'

- **Supporting.**   Giving agreement or support to another person's suggestion.
  'Yes, that's a good idea, I'm sure it would work.'

- **Disagreeing**   Giving a reasoned disagreement with another person's idea or suggestion.
  'I don't think it would work because of the timescale.'

- **Clarifying**. Giving further information to clarify something said previously.
'What I meant by timescale is that we have to submit the report by this Friday.'

- **Summarising**. Identifying the points already discussed or agreed.
'So far we have agreed that Peter will prepare the graphs and Sue will go to the library for more information.'

- **Testing understanding**. Establishing either other people's or your own understanding of previous contributions made.
'Am I right in believing that we will meet again on Tuesday?'

- **Bringing in**. A direct or positive attempt to involve other members of the team.
'Chris, is there anything you would like to add at this stage?'

- **Harmonising**. Attempting to reconcile disagreements or reducing conflict.
'That's an interesting point Mike, what makes you say that?'

Negative behaviours

- **Blocking**. Disagreeing without giving a reason.
'That wouldn't work.'

- **Shutting out**. Interrupting, or talking over another person and thus excluding them from the discussion.

- **Defending/ attacking**. Defending your position or attacking another person's ideas often with emotional overtones.
'You never agree with my ideas.' 'That's just plain stupid.'

A further behaviour often used which is neither positive nor negative is:

- **Open**. This is when a person expresses their lack of knowledge about the subject and may open them-

selves to criticism or even ridicule.
'*I don't really know what we are talking about.*'

Improving your team

Encourage your team to concentrate on the positive behaviours as this will help to make your and their communications more effective and productive and will reduce conflict.

Discourage negative behaviours by asking those who use them, why they did so.

Exercise

In order to help you to recognise the various behaviours, classify the following verbal statements according to the above categories:

1 Why don't we put the lights on?

2 Am I right in thinking that nobody will receive more than 10 per cent?

3 The company won't stand for that.

4 What shall we do next?

5 I like that idea.

6 I think Tom's suggestion would work well if we also added a choice of colours.

7 Let's move on to the next item.

8 It's almost time we left.

9 So far we have agreed the following . . .

10 Shut up unless you have something worth saying.

11 Let me try and explain this further.

12 Have you anything to add, Jane?

13 I don't think that would work because we haven't got the manpower.

14 I suggest we take a break to let everyone calm down.

15 Let me tell you a few home truths.

16 It's no good asking me.

(See Appendix 2 for answers.)

USING THE RIGHT WORDS, TONE AND BODY LANGUAGE

Using words carefully

We have complete control over the words that we use. However, this does not stop us from using words and phrases which may be interpreted quite differently by the listener from the way intended by the speaker. This is often because the tone of voice we use is sending a different message from the words.

At times we intentionally say things to express our disapproval or to get a reaction without fully realising the effect this has on the listener. For example:

- **Criticism**. Nobody likes to hear phrases such as 'That's wrong', 'Why on earth did you do that', 'I won't tell you again.' These will usually result in a defensive response and can lead to arguments. The objective of criticism is to right a wrong such that it is unlikely to recur. So be constructive and try using phrases such as 'Let's have another look at that' or 'How can we improve . . .'

- **Threats**. 'This is your last chance' or 'If you don't buck up your ideas you're out.' The effect on the listener will obviously be increased fear and anxiety.

- **Orders**. Unless specifically trained to accept orders, as in the military, few people respond positively to being ordered to do something. They prefer to be asked.

We may also say things inadvertently or with the best intention, only to be surprised by the response.

- **Reassurance**. Telling people not to worry and everything will be alright without giving reasons can be frustrating to the listener.

- **Advice**. Unsolicited advice is rarely accepted gratefully. 'If I were you I would . . .' Even when asked for, be wary about giving it, for unless it is a genuine request for help, most people only want their solution confirmed, so you have a fifty-fifty chance of being wrong. Before offering advice, first ask the person what their thoughts or views are.

Modifying your tone

We have less control over the tone we use as it is dictated by our feelings about the subject or person we are talking to. Our tone can change depending upon the response we receive. Tone can express feelings such as anger, compassion, sarcasm, happiness, disappointment and so on. It is important to modify your tone so that it is appropriate to the conversation.

By emphasising particular words we can alter the meaning of a sentence. Try saying 'What are you going to do this weekend?' first by emphasising the word *what*, then *you* and finally *this*. There will be three totally different meanings from using exactly the same words.

Although it is important to add colour to our conversations by changing the tone of our voice, try and reduce tones that can be interpreted as being negative by the listener.

Being aware of body language

We have virtually no control over our body language as our expressions, gestures and body movements are purely subconscious. Although we may initially adopt an open, relaxed posture, our body instinctively reacts to what we hear and signals our true feelings and emotions.

It is not possible to explore this subject in depth in this book; suffice it to say that you should watch for changes in people's body language. For example, if the other person suddenly folds their arms or crosses their legs, they may feel threatened by what you have said, so alter your posture or change your tone. On the other hand, if the person begins to rub their chin, they are probably thinking about what you have just said and perhaps coming to a decision, so keep quiet and let them consider.

Several books have been written on body language and are well worth reading to gain a better insight into this fascinating subject.

BEING ASSERTIVE

Assertiveness is the label given to a collection of behaviours which stem from the belief that **your needs and wants are as important as other people's**.

Other recognised behaviours stem from beliefs that your needs or wants are **less** or **more** important than other people's. The former is known as **passive** and the latter as **aggressive**.

The main characteristics of **assertive behaviour** are as follows:

1. Use 'I' statements rather than 'you' statements.
   'You always interrupt me when I am talking.' (aggressive)
   'I have something very important to tell you, so listen carefully and save your questions till the end.' (assertive)

2. Use factual descriptions instead of judgements.
   'Your work is appalling.' (aggressive)
   'I need to see an improvement in your work to enable us to reach our objectives.' (assertive)

3. Acknowledge ownership of your own feelings and emotions
   'You make me so mad.' (denies ownership)
   'I feel very frustrated when you refuse to work as part of the team.' (acknowledges ownership)

4. Use clear and direct requests when wanting something done.
   'Would you mind sending this to Julie?'' (passive)
   'Will you send this to Julie please?' (assertive)

5. When refusing a request, give a reason and an option.
   'No, I don't really have time now.' (passive)
   'No way.' (aggressive)
   'No, because I have this work to finish by 5.00pm. However, I will do it tomorrow morning.' (assertive)

6. When expressing views and opinions, give reasons for your comments.
   'I don't really like that idea, do you?' (passive)
   'I don't agree with that because it would exceed our budget.' (assertive)

7. Use a neutral, non-emotional tone of voice. Often when people think they are being assertive, their tone of voice is interpreted as being aggressive.

It is recommended that you only use assertive techniques when necessary. Overuse could label you as being a cold fish and after all, everyone needs to express their emotions sometimes.

GIVING INSTRUCTIONS

As the leader of a team, there will be times when you have to give instructions or directions to individuals or the team as a whole. To ensure that any such instructions are fully understood:

- think carefully about what you want to say

- be clear

- be concise

- be assertive

- test understanding by asking the listeners 'Have I made myself clear?' and inviting questions or if necessary asking the recipients to repeat back the instructions.

It is vitally important to make sure that instructions are understood correctly as this will save time that would otherwise be wasted by misunderstanding or misinterpretation.

IMPROVING LISTENING SKILLS

There are two sides to every oral communication, talking and listening. The latter is often very difficult as we have never been taught to listen. We hear a great deal but do we really listen?

Here are a few tips to help you to improve your listening skills:

- **Preparing yourself to listen**. Get into the right mental attitude and think about what the speaker is trying to say.

- **Maintaining eye contact**. Look at the speaker and show that you are listening. There is nothing more annoying when you are talking to someone and you see their eyes wandering round the room, apparently looking for something more interesting than you.

- **Keeping an open mind**. Avoid making assumptions or jumping to conclusions as they may prevent you from hearing the facts or truth. Don't feel threatened by messages which may contradict your beliefs, ideas and values. You never know, you may actually learn something.

- **Resisting distractions**. Don't welcome interruptions or carry on signing letters or working out your expenses.

- **Encouraging the speaker**. Invite the speaker to continue by nodding and using words like 'Yes', 'Really', 'I see'.

- **Reflecting back**. Identify specific words that the speaker uses such as boring, exciting, annoying, happy. Repeat the word back to the speaker – this will show that you have listened to what has been said and encourage them to elaborate.

- **Holding back**. Don't be tempted to interrupt. Give the speaker time to collect their thoughts.

- **Concentrate**. Last but by no means least, concentrate on what is being said and clear your mind of all other thoughts.

Practise these techniques and your listening will improve.

CASE STUDIES

Nigel does not encourage communication

Nigel's idea of communication is to give orders, issue threats and criticise performance. As he rarely meets with his staff, most communication is via the telephone. Knowing the type of response they will get, the salespeople avoid making contact as much as possible and dread the sound of the telephone between 6.00pm and 7.00pm which is the time he chooses to phone them. Most conversations are one-way with Nigel doing all the talking.

As a result the 'team' are frustrated and demotivated and Nigel has no idea how they really feel – not that he would care.

Sue believes in good communication

Sue does everything possible to encourage her team to exchange information and ideas. She holds regular meetings at which she poses problems for open discussion. Sue is particularly keen to ensure that the personnel officers and the trainers talk to each other. Whenever she detects any negative behaviours, she makes it her duty to have a quiet chat with the person concerned to discover the reason.

Sue has proved that good communication helps the team to help each other and achieve its goals.

Tom is having a few problems

Coming from a military background, Tom is used to giving and receiving orders and is finding it difficult to adopt what he would call a 'soft' approach to communication. His team do not respond well to orders and prefer to be asked to do something.

The difference in age between Tom and his team is also proving to be a problem. He is having to listen and realise that his players have ideas and suggestions which could be useful in helping them to play as a team.

SUMMARY

- Good communication between team members is a vital ingredient in promoting good teamwork.

- Reduce the barriers to good communication as much as possible.

- Encourage good communication behaviours and eliminate the negative ones. This will help the team move forward together.

- Use tone and body language appropriate to the message.

- Be assertive as and when necessary.

- Give instructions clearly and concisely.

- Listen carefully – it's the only way to discover what the speaker is saying and you might learn something.

- Encourage the team to talk to each other.

6
Handling Discontent within the Team

Despite your best efforts, it is very unlikely that you will totally avoid all tensions and conflict in your team. Therefore you need to be aware of the possible causes and be able to deal with it as quickly as possible.

ANALYSING THE CAUSES

There are numerous possible causes for discontent within your team, including the following:

Your leadership style
Do you always adopt the style appropriate to the individuals, the team and the situation? If people do not believe that they are being led in the manner that they expect, they can become demotivated which in turn can lead to conflict.

Interpersonal conflict
The main reasons for this are:

- One person continually 'cherry-picking' all the good jobs.

- An individual promoting their own interests at the expense of the team.

- The team believing that one of their colleagues is not pulling their weight or performing to the accepted standard.

- Personal dislike of an individual by others due to their attitude.

Insufficient resources
When people believe that they do not have enough equipment, consumables, space, time or information to do their jobs, they can become irritable and blame you and/or the company. Similarly, if the machinery that they use continually breaks down.

Shortage of skills
If the team have not been sufficiently trained to carry out their tasks, they will feel pressurised and pass the blame for their shortcomings onto others including you.

Changes
The longer a team is in existence, the more likely there are to be changes. These may be due to external or internal influences resulting in alterations to the targets or working practices. Team members may leave and others join. Although most people do not mind change, they do mind being changed. Therefore all changes need to be handled carefully and too many can cause discontent among the team.

Lack of discipline
Every team needs a set of rules and a degree of discipline to give itself a structure. If team members believe that you as their leader are not exercising sufficient control over the behaviour and activities of others, conflict may be the result.

Low performance standards
If poor performance appears to be acceptable, those team members who aspire to higher standards will become disenchanted with their low performing colleagues. If good performance is not recognised, people will become demotivated.

Lack of creativity
Every team needs creativity and innovation. Do you encourage new ideas? Do you 'yes but ...' every suggestion made by the team? Teams can become very frustrated if none or very few of their ideas are acted upon.

Lack of team spirit
If the individuals think that, because of their individual skills and tasks, they do not need to be a team, yet feel forced into behaving like one, it can have a detrimental effect on their performance.

Complaining
Most people like to have something to grumble about, be it salaries, working conditions, lack of promotional prospects, the company or whatever. It is your task to make sure that this does not get out of hand and affect the team's performance.

Stress

There are numerous causes for stress. However, two of the most common reasons in the workplace are feeling overworked or underworked. In the first instance, when people feel unable to cope with their workload they become stressed due to the fact that they believe that you and/or the company will look upon it as a sign of weakness. As a result their work will suffer and their behaviour will change. They will look for excuses and blame others, including you, for their poor performance.

Equally, when people feel that they are not being stretched or given the opportunity to utilise their skills and abilities to their full potential, frustration can set in, they become bored and discontented, with results similar to the above.

DEALING WITH THE SYMPTOMS

Your leadership style

Refer back to Chapter 2. Remember, leadership is about being flexible in the way that you handle different situations. Different members of your team will expect you to be one or more of the following:

- *controller* who issues specific instructions and directions and closely supervises their work

- *guide* who clarifies the tasks and offers help to achieve them

- *consultant* who outlines the tasks and invites ideas and discussion as to the best way forward with everyone's agreement

- *facilitator* who, while giving overall direction, delegates responsibilities to the team.

Always remember that you are part of the team.

Interpersonal conflict

You may need to delegate tasks to ensure a fair distribution of the good jobs.

If you suspect any conflict between team members, stand back and take a good look at the behaviour that is taking place before acting. Talk to the people concerned and question them to find out the cause of the problem. Whenever possible get those involved to talk it through, in your presence, to reach an amicable solution. Members of a team do not have to like each other to be effective.

Look at some of the exercises in Appendix 1, particularly numbers

1, 2, 3 and 7, and consider using one or more of these at a team meeting or training session. They may well highlight instances of interpersonal conflict and open the way for possible resolutions.

Insufficient resources

It is your responsibility as the leader to ensure that there are enough resources to meet the targets. Because you are not always at the 'coal face' you will not always be aware of what is required. Educate your team to let you know what is needed, be it new equipment, photocopy paper, time, information or whatever. It is then up to you to provide it. You may wish to delegate to one of your team the responsibility of reordering consumables up to a fixed value. Obviously where capital equipment is involved, the cost of which is outside your budget, you will have to make a case for such expenditure to your manager/director.

If your team is using machinery which is nearing the end of its life, institute a preventative maintenance system to reduce the likelihood of breakdowns.

Shortage of skills

If there is a shortage of skill because of someone leaving or changes in work practice, you will need either to train existing members of your team or buy in the necessary skills.

Changes

Goals and objectives may change because of external factors such as changes in customer demand, new technology, legal or economic changes and so on. The reasons may be internal; for example, new product development, reorganisations or the introduction of new systems. Whatever the reason, you need to explain the changes and how it will affect your team at the earliest opportunity. Discuss with your team how best to implement any such changes.

Lack of discipline

Ensure that everyone knows what is expected of them in terms of their behaviour. Deal with each case of indiscipline fairly and equally and be seen to be doing so.

Low performance standards

Set standards of behaviour, quality and quantity. Re-emphasise them as often as necessary and help those falling below these standards to achieve them by providing the required training on a one-to-one basis. If certain people believe that the standards are too low, stretch them by giving them higher targets or delegating more demanding tasks.

Don't forget to praise efforts as well as results.

Lack of creativity

It is your responsibility as the team leader to create the right atmosphere to encourage ideas and innovation. Make it known that you are always open to suggestions from your team. Don't dismiss ideas out of hand; consider each one carefully, for although a particular suggestion may not be practical it could be the stimulus you need to get other creative ideas flowing.

If your team appear reticent in coming up with ideas, include a brainstorm session as part of a team meeting. This will help to focus people's minds on being creative and the benefits that can result.

Lack of team spirit

If there are no real benefits to be gained from working as a team, then don't force it. You must be the judge. It will then be a matter of managing each individual towards the overall goal.

Complaining

It is part of everyone's nature to complain about something so there is no need to worry unless it becomes disruptive. In that case, call a team meeting, identify the causes of the complaints and ask for ideas on how to overcome them. Some may be resolvable, others not, but at least it gets them into the open and demonstrates that you acknowledge that they exist.

Stress

Your task is to reduce the causes of stress as much as possible. Do not over-delegate to your team. Eliminate all unnecessary jobs. Be prepared to roll up your sleeves and help out. Train the team to prioritise their tasks and manage their time effectively. Resist unacceptable pressure from above by being assertive to your boss. Make sure that everyone is occupied and develop people to accept more responsibility where practical. Lead by example and watch your own stress level.

CASE STUDIES

Nigel believes conflict is part of the job

Being competitive by nature, Nigel believes that conflict is healthy and keeps people on their toes. He is only interested in achieving his targets and doesn't mind how they are reached. He sets performance standards and expects them to be adhered to, criticising anyone who fails. Nigel resists any ideas and suggestions from his salespeople and ignores their complaints. Although he is aware that many of his 'team' are discontented, his philosophy is that if they don't like it they can leave. The high turnover of personnel under his control has been noted.

Sue is concerned about conflict

Sue does everything possible to reduce discontent within her team. She sets standards, makes sure that all the required skills and resources are available, encourages ideas and does everything in her power to provide an enjoyable working environment.

When Sue notices that two of her trainers appear to be having a heated discussion, she steps in to find out the cause. Apparently one trainer is accusing the other of hogging too much of the training administrator's time. She discusses it with the trainers and the administrator and the problem is quickly resolved.

Tom learns to handle conflict

Tom notices that whenever the teams lose a match, the forwards blame the backs and vice versa. He quickly realises that the reason for this is because the two factions do not appreciate each other's problems. In an attempt to resolve this, he arranges a practice match putting the backs into the scrum and playing the forwards as backs. By playing out of their normal positions, the players soon understand the difficulties involved. As a result, when they revert to their original positions, the players work together as a more effective unit and any blame is shared equally.

SUMMARY

- Conflict is part of the teambuilding process.
- Analyse the possible causes.
- Reduce the likelihood of conflict by:
  - using the most appropriate leadership styles

- ensuring that the team have the right skills and sufficient resources

- setting standards of quality and behaviour

- encouraging a good team spirit

- reducing the causes of stress.

- Deal with all conflicts as quickly as possible; do not let them fester.

- Discuss unacceptable behaviour with the person or persons concerned to resolve the problem.

7
Training the Team

As the manager of the team, you will be concerned with two types of training: firstly, training to ensure that everyone has the necessary skills and knowledge to perform their jobs to the expected standard; and secondly, training to work as an efficient team.

As this book is about building teams, we will concentrate on the latter.

COMPARING THE TYPES OF TRAINING AVAILABLE

Team training can be undertaken either externally or within the company or department.

External training

Courses
There are numerous external training courses available, some good, others less so. If you intend to use an external course, find out as much about it as you can and if possible talk to someone who has attended. It is only then that you can judge whether or not it is suitable for your team's needs.

These courses normally consist of a series of exercises designed to be undertaken by teams of delegates with the aim of improving teamwork.

There is little point in sending only one of your team on such a course for whereas they may work very well with their fellow delegates, the object is to work with their colleagues back at the workplace. Also, if only one person is selected for the course, the rest of the team will wonder why they were not chosen. Therefore, if you decide to use this form of training, make sure everyone attends, preferably in twos or threes.

These courses are usually 3 to 5 days in duration and can therefore be quite expensive, upwards of £500 plus any accommodation necessary.

Adventure/Outward Bound training

For anyone not familiar with this form of training, it consists of sending delegates to a remote part of the British Isles where they will live in rather spartan conditions and be expected to undertake a number of outdoor activities such as abseiling, canoeing, raft building, rock climbing, trekking and so on. The aim is that, by doing activities that are very different from those that they encounter at work, participants will improve their interpersonal and teamworking skills.

This type of training has proved popular with many companies but sometimes less so with many of the employees sent to them, particularly if they are not physically fit.

Much emphasis is placed on feedback from the course leaders. These courses are often staffed by ex-military personnel who sometimes forget that they are no longer in the forces and their methods can be construed as over-critical and aggressive. As a result, certain delegates can become very upset and demotivated. One example is where a group were instructed to make their way to a certain rendezvous, where a hot breakfast would await them. The group spent the night trekking over moorland, wading through streams and swimming across an icy cold lake. When they arrived totally exhausted and wet through, they were told by the course leader, with a sadistic grin on his face, that someone had forgotten to bring any food. Not surprisingly everyone gave full vent to their feelings, left the course and went home.

Once again, look very carefully into each programme before using them. How would your team react to this type of training?

One-day training

A number of training providers offer one-day programmes. The idea is to send one or more complete teams from a company to improve their team skills by performing exercises that have nothing to do with their work. This enables them to concentrate on the team skills and can be very effective. A number of such courses consist of exercises similar to those used on longer courses, whilst others concentrate on outdoor activities such as completing obstacle courses or 'paintball' warfare.

Internal training

Courses

If your company has a training department, they may already offer courses on teambuilding. Check them out as they may be suitable for your team.

Consultants

There are a number of good, independent training consultants who will visit your company and run full or half-day teambuilding courses. Not only will they be experienced in providing the right training, but being from outside the company will add credibility and importance to the training.

The average cost is £400 to £500 per day. It is not recommended that you pay more as higher fees will certainly not mean better training. You may be able to spread this cost by sharing the day with another team from your company.

You

You are in the best position to decide what training your team needs. It is not necessary for you to be an experienced trainer to provide the required training or to incorporate simple teambuilding exercises as part of your team meetings.

DECIDING WHAT TRAINING IS REQUIRED

As mentioned earlier in this book, one of the best ways of determining what training is needed is by observation and noting those areas that require improvement. Normally, team training falls into one or more of the following categories:

- **Communicating**. As we have already seen, good communication is the key to good teamworking. Are your team talking to each other? Are they listening? Is the right information being communicated? Are the right questions being asked? Does the communication bring the desired results? A 'no' answer to any of these questions means that some training would be beneficial to all concerned.

- **Co-operating**. Teamworking is all about co-operation between the members. Is everyone working towards the same goals? Do your team help and support each other? Does everyone share information? Again, any negative answers will provide you with the opportunity to provide training.

- **Involving**. It is important that everyone has the chance to become involved in all aspects of the team. Are the team involved in solving problems and making decisions? Do they make suggestions for improvements? Does everyone contribute to team meetings? If not, maybe they do not know how to or what is expected of them. A short training session will help to overcome such obstacles.

There may well be other areas such as planning, innovating and time management which could form the basis of a training session.

PLANNING THE TRAINING

Having decided upon the objective of the training, the next thing is to decide how to do it.

Exercises

Every member of your team should be involved in the training, therefore the best and simplest way for you to present the training is in the form of team exercises. To help you, a selection of easy-to-run exercises have been included in Appendix 1 of this book.

Videos

There are a number of videos relating to team work which are available for hire or purchase. These are accompanied by a booklet which provides a guide as to the most effective method of using them as a training aid.

PREPARING THE TRAINING SESSION

If you intend using a video, follow the booklet. However, if you propose to use an exercise:

- Select the most suitable exercise for your purpose.

- Familiarise yourself with it thoroughly by reading it through several times.

- Prepare your introduction and explanation.

- Decide how the team should feed back their results.

- Collect all necessary equipment, flip chart, handouts and so on.

DELIVERING THE TRAINING EXERCISES

It is suggested that initially the exercises should be an extension of team meetings, at least until the team becomes used to this type of training.

- Explain how the exercise works, the objective and method of feedback.

- Invite questions for clarification.

- Distribute all equipment and handouts.

- Set the timescale.

- Observe the team working and make notes. You should be more concerned with the process (how the team work together) than the result.

- Ask the team for their feedback and add your observations.

ASSESSING THE TRAINING

At the conclusion of each exercise, ask every member of the team to write brief notes on what they gained from it and how they felt the team operated. This will give you valuable information which can be used in any future training.

You should observe each exercise and note such matters as:

- Were roles, e.g. time-keeper, co-ordinator, spokesperson, delegated and taken on?

- Did everyone become involved?

- What leadership style was adopted, if any?

- How well did the team operate as a unit?

- Was there any conflict? If so, how was it handled?

KEEPING A RECORD

It is a good idea to keep a simple record of the exercises or videos that you have used, together with comments on their effectiveness. (See Figure 3.)

TRAINING RECORD		
Exercise/Video	**Date used**	**Comments**
Tower Project	**x/x/xx**	**Worked well, object achieved**

Fig. 3. Training record.

CASE STUDIES

Nigel keeps training to a minimum

As we have already seen, Nigel is not an advocate of team work so would not consider training necessary. He also believes that the best way to develop individual skills is by criticism. The only training that he provides is when a new product is introduced. In such cases, he calls his group together, hands out details and brochures of the product and tells them what their targets are.

Training is important to Sue

Sue is a great believer in team training as in her opinion it helps to keep the team together. The type of training that she favours is an exercise as part of a team meeting. Having trainers in her team, it would be simple for her to ask one of them to run the training. However, to broaden the development of the whole team, she invites a different person to take each session. Sue pays particular attention to good, constructive feedback. Because of her positive attitude, the team look forward to taking part in the exercises.

Training is vital for Tom's teams

Tom knows the importance of training, so at the beginning of the season he distributes a training schedule to each member of the squads. There are two team training sessions every week, after school hours, lasting one hour each. Tom plans each session carefully to include both individual skills and team work. He tries to make the training enjoyable as he believes that the players will train harder if they enjoy it. Occasionally Tom uses a training video to illustrate certain points.

Because Tom believes that training is such an important ingredient to the success of the team, if a player misses a session for any reason apart from injury or illness, he is unlikely to be selected for the next match.

SUMMARY

- The leader/manager is responsible for ensuring that the team is trained.

- Decide where training is required.

- Choose the most appropriate method from the options available.

- Incorporate team training exercises into team meetings.

- Evaluate each training session.

- Keep simple training records.

- Make the training enjoyable for the participants.

- Regular, ongoing training is more effective than the occasional one-off fix.

8
Assessing your Team

While it is common practice to review performance at the conclusion of a project or upon achieving specific objectives, it is equally important to monitor the progress of your team on an ongoing basis. This will enable you to make adjustments if necessary before it is too late.

MONITORING YOUR TEAM

To monitor your team's performance accurately, you will need to establish measurable standards or yardsticks at the outset. This is comparatively simple with quantifiable matters such as timescale, budget, revenue, volume of production and so on. However, it becomes more difficult when attempting to assess how the team works as it cannot be measured in terms of numbers or specifications. You will have formed an impression of what makes a team successful and that is the best quality standard you can define. This is sometimes referred to as the 'elephant test'. It is almost impossible to describe an elephant but you know what it looks like and you would recognise one when you saw it.

When monitoring or reviewing your team performance, there are three questions which need answers.

1. Where are we now?

2. Where should we be?

3. How do we get there?

You may have answers to these questions, but are they the same as your team's? Part of the monitoring process should include team meetings where everyone has a chance to air their views.

INVOLVING YOUR TEAM

To provide a structure for a team review meeting, start by asking everyone to complete a Team Progress Sheet which can be something along the lines of the example in Figure 4. Having collated this information, you will have the team's answer to the first question, 'Where are we now?', which can be the starting point for the meeting. The team should now decide where they should be. Ideally this will be excellent in all areas. However, is this realistic? The sensible aim should be to improve by one or two points before the next review.

TEAM PROGRESS SHEET	
Please rate the following on a scale of 1–5, with 1 being excellent and 5 very poor.	
Everyone knows exactly what the team's objectives are.	
The team have all the skills required to achieve the objectives.	
Everyone is open and honest with each other.	
People help one another and work together as a team.	
Team meetings help us to operate as a real team.	
Information is sought and given as required.	
The leadership style is participatory and not autocratic.	
The team is able to solve problems and make decisions.	
Conflict is kept to a minimum	

Fig. 4. Example of a team progress chart.

The next problem to discuss is what needs to be done to reach each goal. A 'brainstorm' can be a very useful way of gathering possible solutions. Finally, agree Action Plans for the next meeting.

Beware of complacency. Just because your team has achieved its targets, it does not necessarily follow that they are a 'successful team' – they could have been lucky on this occasion. The question is 'Could they do it again?' There is always room for improvement.

Every management system from Total Quality Management to Just-In-Time depends upon teams maintaining high standards. Quality is about continuous improvement.

GETTING YOUR TEAM TO APPRAISE EACH OTHER

This can produce some very useful and interesting information on how the members of your team perceive their colleagues. Your views about a particular individual may be quite different from that of their team mates. Although some managers may consider this to be a high risk exercise, if it is carried out correctly it should not be a problem.

- Ask each person to write down positive and negative attributes for each of their colleagues. One sheet of paper for each person.

- The strict rule is that there must be at least three positives for every one negative.

- Collect the papers and analyse the information.

- You may then wish to have a brief, private meeting with each person to discuss the comments relating to them and consider what steps can be taken to make any improvements necessary.

CASE STUDIES

Nigel only make quantitative assessments
When assessing his salespeople, Nigel is only interested in the revenue and profit made by each person. He has no idea of what the 'team' think of each other and quite frankly he could not care less. He is judged on his team's results, so as far as he is concerned, figures are the only way to assess the performance of the individuals.

Sue regularly monitors her team's performance
An important part of every one of Sue's team meetings is a review of past performance and a discussion on how to make improvements.

Because her team knows this, they are continually striving to come up with ideas on how to increase their efficiency as a team.

Tom holds post-match reviews
Immediately after each match, Tom conducts a brief dressing-room meeting to discuss what went right and what went wrong. Before airing his views, he invites comments from the team. The meetings conclude with a list of things to be practised at the next training session.

SUMMARY

- Set measurable standards where possible.

- Monitor team performance at regular intervals.

- Assess the qualitative as well as quantitative areas.

- Involve the team in establishing where they are.

- Discuss with the team where they should be and how to get there.

- Conclude each meeting with Action Plans and interim targets.

- Ask the team to appraise their colleagues.

Appendix 1
Team Exercises

These well-tried and tested exercises can easily be run by you for your team.

Read through each one carefully to familiarise yourself with the details before using them.

Each one has been designed to enable your team to practise different aspects of team working.

Exercise 1 – What Time Is it?
Sharing information to answer a question.

Exercise 2 – The Tower Project
Working together to achieve a given objective.

Exercise 3 – The Flying Egg
Solving a practical problem with a competitive element.

Exercise 4 – People Problems
Solving problems as a team from given information.

Exercise 5 – The Rescue
Making team decisions.

Exercise 6 – Self-Organisation
Planning and time management.

Exercise 7 – Team Problem-Solving
Illustrating the benefits of solving problems as a team.

Exercise 8 – Multi-Task Management
Planning, allocating resources, problem-solving and team management.

EXERCISE 1 – WHAT TIME IS IT?

Objective: This exercise is designed to provide the team with practice in exchanging information to answer a question and to differentiate between relevant and irrelevant information.

Material: 1 set of statement cards.

Timing: 15 minutes to answer the question.
10 minutes feedback.

Running the exercise

1. Before you can run this exercise you will need to write each statement, including the question, on a separate card (see list below).

2. Seat the team round a table and explain the exercise and its purpose.

3. Using the information they are given they must answer the question and adhere to the following rules:

   • Nothing must be written down.

   • Cards must not be shown to other team members.

   • All questions must be addressed to individuals only.

4. Distribute the cards to the team as equally as possible.

5. Do not appoint a leader. Observe the proceedings of the team.

6. At the end of 15 minutes, the team must give their answer and identify all irrelevant information.

7. Feedback your observations and comments.

Question
What is the time in Amberville?

Statements
Bealtown is on Greenwich Mean Time.

Colbrooke is directly south of Bealtown.

Dunbridge is four hours behind Bealtown.

Amberville is one hour ahead of Dunbridge.

The time by the Town Hall clock in Colbrooke is 7.15 pm.

Amberville uses the 24-hour clock.

The population of Ealham is 40,541.

The main crop in Dunbridge is maize.

Bealtown buys all its maize from Dunbridge.

Everyone in Amberville over 18 owns a watch.

Dunbridge holds its maize auction each day at noon.

The flight time from Amberville to Forford is one hour.

Bealtown has a curfew between 9.00 pm and 6.00 am.

The clocks in Amberville go forward one hour in the summer.

Tomorrow will be 27 January.

By tradition the clocks in Colbrooke are always one hour slow.

Amberville is not in the southern hemisphere.

Forford is north of Ealham.

The people in Ealham do not eat maize.

Answer
The correct time in Amberville is 17.15 hours.

EXERCISE 2 – THE TOWER PROJECT

Objectives: – To practise the basic principles of time management and the achievement of an agreed objective through working together as a team.

Materials: – 50 sheets of standard A4 copier paper.
1 roll of adhesive tape.
Flip chart.

Handouts: – Tower Project Brief.
Feedback Form.
Effective Objectives.
Systematic Working.

Timing: – 45 minutes to get the task completed.
15 minutes for the feedback.

Running the exercise

1. Nominate a team leader who is responsible for ensuring the successful completion of the task. Everyone is given a copy of the Tower Project Brief to read.

2. Having given the team a few minutes to read the brief, state that the '60 minutes starts now.' You can either take on the role of time-keeper yourself or delegate the task to one of the team.

3. When the tower has been built, measure the height and determine the score so that the achievement can be evaluated against the objectives.

4. Distribute a copy of the Feedback Form to every team member and ask them to complete it. You should also complete the form.

5. Once this has been completed, invite a discussion based on the feedback.

6. Write the positive points on the flip chart and identify those areas that need improvement.

7. Finally distribute the Effective Objectives and Systematic Working handouts and talk through them.

THE TOWER PROJECT BRIEF

The purpose of the task is to plan the time available in order to build a free-standing paper tower using only the materials provided (50 sheets of A4 copier paper) and the resources of the team.

1. You have 60 minutes to complete the task including planning, execution and review. You have complete freedom in the way the first 45 minutes is used but the final 15 minutes must be allocated to the feedback session. You should aim to have a visible and agreed outline time plan within 10 minutes of the start.

2. Only the paper provided may be used during the planning and construction phases. Any paper used prior to the actual construction phase cannot be reused and must be scrapped.

3. One of the measures of success is the score achieved using the following formula:

$$\frac{\text{Height of tower in centimetres}}{\text{No of sheets used} \times \text{Time taken rounded up to the nearest minute}}$$

4. 10 is considered a reasonable score for the task.

PAPER TOWER PROJECT – FEEDBACK FORM

Team leader:..
Team: ....
Reviewer:...

Questions	Notes and examples
1. What were the team objectives for the task and were they achieved?	
2. Was an affective time plan established making it clear who was going to do what, when and where and how progress and time-scales would be monitored? Were the whole team aware of the plan?	
3. Were individual skills identified and utilised and did they work well as a team?	
4. How was the team organised? Was it conducive to effective communication within the group?	
5. Was there a sense of purpose, urgency and involvement with the task and if not how could this be achieved?	
6. What was the balance of participation? Was everybody involved?	
7. How well were difficult situations handled (including disagreements) and did the team leader maintain effective control throughout the task? Was understanding and agreement checked?	
8. What was the leadership style and was it appropriate for the task? To what extent did the team leader contribute to or work against the achievement of task objectives?	

Summary of strengths and improvement plan

PAPER TOWER PROJECT – EFFECTIVE OBJECTIVES

Introduction
Objectives are not easy to define. It takes time and self-discipline to identify what has to be achieved. It is, however, time well spent, as defining the objectives of the task or project will instill the discipline of effective planning.

What is an objective?
It is a description of what we want to achieve.

Why use objectives?
By specifying objectives at an early stage of a task/project it makes us consider the following:

- timescales

- the task to be achieved

- standards that need to be met

- the resources available.

This in turn forces us to **plan** better.

What makes an objective effective?
It must be:

- clear and unambiguous

- relevant

- realistic

- measurable

- agreed.

Format for setting objectives
- By (when?) (who?).

- Will have (done what?) (to what standard?).

- With the aid of (what resources?).

PAPER TOWER PROJECT – SYSTEMATIC WORKING

A systematic approach to getting things done

1. **Purpose**
   Identify the purpose of the task.

2. **Objectives**
   Establish clear, realistic, relevant and measurable objectives which take into account time, materials, manpower, money and the nature of the work to be done.

3. **Information**
   Collect all information relating to the task and the objectives.

4. **Review**
   Use the information to identify all the tasks that need to be planned.

5. **Plan**
   Plan the tasks that need to be performed specifying who will do what, when and where. Build in agreed check points.

6. **Action**
   Action the plan.

7. **Performance improvement**
   Review the achievements against the objectives identifying improvements that can be made for future activities.

Between stages 1 and 6 a continuous monitoring function should be performed and where necessary earlier stages can be re-entered.

EXERCISE 3 – THE FLYING EGG

Objectives: To work together as a team to achieve the objective by identifying and using the skills and experience of the team members.

Materials: 2 sheets of flip chart paper.
1 small roll of adhesive tape.
1 metre of string.
1 large elastic band.
1 fresh egg.

Handouts: The Flying Egg Brief.
Feedback sheet.

Timing: 30 minutes to complete the task.
15 minutes for feedback.

Running the exercise

1. Although it has been previously stated that teams should not be competitive within themselves, this exercise benefits from some healthy competition. Therefore divide your team into two groups with a minimum of three people in each. Do not appoint leaders, let them emerge naturally.

2. Give a copy of the Flying Egg Brief to each person to read. Invite any questions for clarification.

3. After a few minutes, distribute a set of materials to each team and tell them that their 30 minutes starts now.

4. At the end of the 30 minutes call 'Time'. Each team is then invited to launch their craft and the distance is measured. Ideally this would take place outside in the car park or similar open space.

5. Give out the feedback sheets and ask everyone to complete one, including yourself.

6. Discuss the exercise paying particular attention to the process. Remember to emphasise that everyone is a winner regardless of the distance flown.

THE FLYING EGG BRIEF

The purpose of this task is to use only the materials supplied and the skills and experience of your team to design and build a craft capable of carrying a fresh egg on a flight through the air as far as possible and land without breaking the egg.

1. You have 30 minutes to complete the task at the end of which time your craft should be ready for launching. You will have a further 15 minutes for feedback.

2. Only the materials supplied can be used for the planning and construction phases. You may reuse the materials as often as required.

3. Upon the completion the craft must be launched by hand from a standing position.

4. To achieve the objective, the craft should travel a minimum of 10 metres and land with the egg unbroken.

EXERCISE 4 – PEOPLE PROBLEMS

Objectives: To discuss various scenarios regarding people problems
and to reach a group solution to the problems and effectively communicate the solutions.

Materials: 4 scenarios.
Feedback forms.

Timing: 30 minutes group discussion.
15 minutes presentation of findings.
15 minutes feedback.

Running the exercise

1. Seat the team around a table and explain the exercise. Distribute
   copies of the scenarios to each person giving them 30 minutes to
   reach solutions to all four.

2. After 30 minutes, invite the team to present their findings. Give
   out the suggested solutions if appropriate.

3. Distribute the feedback sheets and ask the team to complete them
   and discuss the outcome.

SCENARIO 1 – THE MANAGING YOUR MANAGER PROBLEM

You are the team manager of a small development team.

Your boss, the Business Manager, is responsible for approximately 25 staff in three sections. You are the most senior of the three section leaders.

The Business Manager is a brilliant technician with a good reputation throughout the company and tends to spend most of his time attending meetings. Consequently the day-to-day routine administration of the department is handled by yourself. As a result, you are closer to the staff than your boss.

The Business Manager, brilliant and innovative as he is, has a number of faults. His skill in dealing with people is abysmal. He prefers to leave the day-to-day running of the department to his team managers. He sees subordinates as an unfortunate necessity rather than as a team he would like to manage.

Among the criticisms that are being made by more junior staff are:

* He doesn't even know individuals' names.

* He always takes the credit.

* We are just the backroom boys.

* I worked all weekend and didn't even get an acknowledgement.

You are worried, morale is low and staff turnover is increasing. One of the other team leaders has been approached by a head-hunter and is thinking of leaving.

Staff appraisals and development, which work well in other parts of the company and are shortly due, are considered irrelevant by the Business Manager and have therefore been neglected.

You feel that something must be done to get your boss to play a more active and interested role in the running of the department. You have arranged a meeting with him and are now working out your strategy for getting him to improve his skills in dealing with people. Discuss and agree what the approach should be and present the group's findings at the end of 30 minutes.

SCENARIO 2 – THE UNPOPULAR EMPLOYEE PROBLEM

Mike is 23, a graduate recruit into the organisation direct from university. He has attended an induction course and has been allocated to your department for a twelve-month attachment.

Unmarried, he shares a flat with two other people not associated with the company. He hasn't found it easy to adapt to the more conventional way of life after university. He is the only graduate in the team and is an active member of a political party.

At the initial interview he came over as positive and confident but now that he has settled in it is obvious that he has become over-confident to the point of being overbearing. He has started to air his politics more forcibly in the office, starting up political discussions whenever he can to such an extent that the members of the team claim that his continual attempts to involve them in political arguments is distracting them from their work.

Several of them have also mentioned that he has a personal hygiene problem. You know that he goes for a run each morning to keep himself fit but you hadn't noticed the problem yourself.

Mike is doing a good job and you can rely on him to get things done. You do not want to lose him but you are going to have to discuss the situation with him. Discuss your strategy and how you can get Mike back to being an effective team member without upsetting him.

SCENARIO 3 – THE PERFORMANCE DETERIORATION PROBLEM

Jane is 22, left school with 2 A-levels and joined the company as a trainee. She spent two years in other departments and now seems to have settled into your department and is doing very well.

Engaged and planning to get married in three months time, her intention is to continue working after the marriage as they are buying a house. Well liked in the department, she is initially a bit shy but once she gets over it she is friendly and pleasant but never pushy.

She has established herself as a competent and conscientious worker, always carefully checking her work and completing it within the timescales. She has acquired a good knowledge of the work done in the department and has an appreciation of what clients want.

Three weeks ago she started on a small but important job for an old established client and at your review you find that she is seriously behind the time schedule. She seems unconcerned about the situation and it is apparent that she didn't know how far she was behind. She also seemed a bit edgy and from your records you note that she has had several days off giving various reasons – a cold, a visit to the dentist, etc. She has also been making a number of private local telephone calls from the office each day.

You decide that you will have to discuss matters with her in more detail and have arranged a meeting. How would you plan out the meeting? What do you think the real problems are and how can they be resolved?

SCENARIO 4 – THE ILL EMPLOYEE PROBLEM

You are a team manager with eight people reporting to you. John is 28 and has been a team member for 3 years having been recruited by you from another company.

He has always been pleasant and hard working and has got on well with the other members of the team. He has done a very good job, progressing steadily through the grades so that he now has responsibility for the more junior members of the team.

You have noticed that for the past six months he has seemed to be very worried and distinctly off colour. Not that his work has been affected, but he has had more than his usual days off through sickness. You have spoken to him and his reply is that he hasn't been feeling 100 per cent but it isn't interfering with his work and he will make sure that it doesn't. As his work hasn't been affected and he makes up lost time by working late, you have left it that if there is anything you can do to help just to let you know.

Jenny, your second in charge, has asked for a confidential meeting with you and puts it to you that the team are not happy working alongside John. After some probing it transpires that word has got around that John has been confirmed as HIV positive – contracted through a contaminated blood transfusion (Jenny added 'or so he says'). The news has come as a complete surprise to you – what should you do now?

PEOPLE PROBLEMS – FEEDBACK FORM

Team Leader: ....

Team: ....

Reviewer: ....

Questions	Notes and examples
1. What were the team objectives for the task and were they achieved?	
2. Was an effective time plan established making it clear who was going to do what, when and where and how progress and timescales would be monitored? Were the whole team aware of the plan?	
3. Were individual skills indentified and utilised and did they work well as a team?	
4. How was the team organised? Was it conducive to effective communication within the group?	
5. Was there a sense of purpose, urgency and involvement with the task and if not how could this be achieved?	
6. What was the balance of participation? Was everybody involved?	
7. What was the leadership style and was it appropriate for the task? To what extent did the team leader contribute to or work against the achievement of task objectives?	
8. How well did the team leader communicate the team's findings?	

Summary of strengths and improvement plan

People problems – possible solutions

Scenario 1 – The managing your manager problem
The problem would appear to be that the Business Manager is just not interested in people management and is much happier attending meetings and pursuing his technical interests. One solution is to take this up with his manager with a view to getting him replaced by a more people-orientated manager. This could, however, have serious repercussions and you may not get a better person.

The alternative is to get your boss to agree to give the three team leaders more responsibility for the management of the teams, which will also give him more time to pursue his real interests. This should be approached tactfully on the basis that his current workload is not enabling him to devote sufficient time to the management of the teams and with appraisals looming something will need to be done. Giving the team leaders more responsibility, particularly with regard to appraisals, will enable them to take some of the load off his hands.

Scenario 2 – The unpopular employee problem
There are two issues here, the bullying political discussions and the personal hygiene problem.

Both have to be tackled immediately, the first by telling Mike quite firmly that he is not to bring his politics into the workplace as it is disrupting the smooth working of the department.

The personal hygiene problem has to be tackled more tactfully as it could be a consequence of his unpopular political stance. Knowing that he exercises each morning can be used to broach the subject – 'I know that you go for a run each morning and one or two people have remarked that you are a bit sweaty when you come into the office. I haven't noticed it myself and if I did I would say something to you. It is something that should be taken care over and I leave it with you' – or words to that effect. If the personal hygiene problem does continue you have left the door open to remind him.

Scenario 3 – The performance deterioration problem
The most stressful times of your life are getting married, buying a house, having a baby and getting divorced. Jane could be going through all of these (breaking up at this stage is nearly as bad as a divorce). Consider the sort of problems she may have:

- second thoughts about the marriage
- disagreements with her fiancé

- problems with buying the house

- financial problems.

She could even be pregnant!

Or it may be just the normal stress and anxiety of the occasion that is resulting in her work performance deteriorating and it is therefore necessary, if possible, to get her back on track. At this stage you cannot jump to definitive conclusions and you therefore have to arrange a meeting as soon as possible to establish whether she is capable of getting the job done within the timescale. If not it will be necessary to hand it over to somebody else to make sure it is done on time and give her a less demanding task.

Start the meeting on the basis that you were concerned that she is falling behind in her work and that she seems fully preoccupied with her forthcoming marriage. Ask her how everything is progressing and whether she has any significant problems. If she has then it will be necessary to get somebody else to take over her work. If not and it is just the normal pre-marriage activities, emphasise the importance of the work she is doing and ask her if she is going to be able to make up the lost time to bring it back on schedule in addition to all the other activities she is undertaking. If she feels that she can do it get her commitment and draw up a revised plan to get the project back on schedule. Remember that she will be under a lot of pressure over the next three months and only if you are absolutely confident that she will be able to cope with the workload should you let her carry on with the project. It may be necessary to lighten her workload until the pressure is off.

Scenario 4 – The ill employee problem
There are two main issues here

- the legal position regarding discrimination in the workplace

- the people problems in convincing people that it is safe to work alongside individuals who have tested HIV positive.

The legal position is quite clear but it is human nature that some people will refuse to work with a person with HIV even though it is not considered a contagious disease. If people do accept this that is ideal. However, the personnel department will have to become involved in resolving the problems and it could also involve counselling.

In this age of high technology one way it can be resolved is by getting the affected person to work from home. This may not completely satisfy the legal position but could be a good compromise.

EXERCISE 5 – THE RESCUE

Objective: The purpose of this exercise is for the team to make a number of decisions based upon information given to them.

Materials: The Rescue Brief.
Feedback sheets.
Flip chart.

Timing: 30 minutes to complete the exercise.
15 minutes feedback.

Running the exercise

1. Seat the team around a table and explain the exercise and the objectives.
2. Distribute the Brief to each member and tell them that the 30 minutes starts immediately.
3. At the end of 30 minutes, invite the team to feed back their conclusions and reasons.
4. Distribute the feedback sheets and ask each person to complete one and discuss the findings.

THE RESCUE BRIEF

Six people are on board a yacht which is drifting out of control in very heavy seas. The local Air-Sea Rescue have been alerted and have sent a helicopter to pick up the crew. However, it is possible that they will not be able to rescue everyone. Your team represent Base Control and it is your task to decide within the next 30 minutes, the order in which the people will be rescued. Brief character profiles have been provided to help you.

Mary Thomas
Mary is 36, divorced with two children under 10. She is a trained nurse and works part-time at a local hospital. She is a keep-fit enthusiast and runs a local aerobics class. Mary is a well-known, popular figure in her local community.

David Morton
David is 52, married with three grown-up children. He is a scientist currently involved in genetic engineering to provide more nutritious food for the destitute people of Central Africa. He is a leading authority in his field but is notoriously bad at keeping written notes of his work.

Pierre Lefevre
Pierre is a 49-year-old French businessman who moved to Britain 20 years ago and set up a factory near Newcastle. In five days time he will sign a contract which will secure the jobs of 120 people for the next three years. He is happily married and enjoys playing golf when he gets the time.

Toto Yakamoto
Toto is the 20-year-old daughter of a wealthy Japanese industrialist whose company is considering opening a factory in the UK. Toto is studying politics at Oxford University. She has represented her country at table tennis and is an accomplished flower arranger.

Prunella Barrington-Greene
Prunella is 25, unmarried and lives with another young woman in Chelsea. Her father owns the yacht. She is trying to become an actress but has had little success so far. She is a well-known party-goer and her photograph has appeared in numerous society magazines.

Roger Wilton
Roger is an ex-SAS sergeant who now runs an Outward Bound school with his two partners. Although married with three children, he also has a mistress or two. He is a friend of Prunella's father and skipper of the yacht. Roger is a very strong-willed, determined character.

After 30 minutes you will be asked to present your conclusions and give the reasons for the decision.

EXERCISE 6 – SELF-ORGANISATION WORKSHOP

Objectives: To put into practice the basic principles of time management related to the real-life working environment.
Timing: 30 minutes.

Running the workshop
Read through the brief and formulate an outline plan for the day based on the information given. When you are satisfied that everything has been covered, read through the suggested solution, relate it to your own solution and where necessary modify to satisfy your own requirements.

Brief
You arrive back at the office at 8.45 am having had a two-day break. Checking your diary you note that you have a meeting with Stephen Spencer of Personnel at 11.00 am to review the new appraisal procedures (in his office) and you have allowed 45 minutes for the meeting. You have also arranged a follow-up meeting with your team (5 people) in your office at 2.15 pm in order to brief them on the forthcoming appraisals.

Claire Cuthbert, a team member, is also having birthday drinks in the local pub which is 5 minutes walk away between 12.30 and 2.00 pm. You have already confirmed that you will go along. There is also the usual scheduled fortnightly progress meeting with your boss at 4.00 pm in his office. This will take 45 minutes.

Sifting through your in-tray you see the following:

* 3 copies of your monthly trade magazine

* an internal bulletin regarding organisational changes

* a message to ring Valerie Singleton of Trade Educational Services; you use them regularly and have a course booked starting next week for one of the team

* a message to ring Janet Martin on (01626) 664422 (you have never heard of her)

* a letter from Personnel regarding the forthcoming appraisals

* a note from Howard Johnson, one of the team, asking for a quick review of the project he is working on

* several messages to ring Arthur Stanley, Head of Finance

- a message to ring Mrs Wright at the social club regarding the inter-departmental darts match at 7.30 pm; this had been delegated to you by your boss and all the arrangements are in hand

- various circulars regarding exhibitions, training courses, etc.

- the internal circulation file that goes to all team managers and which has been in your tray since Monday

- Stewart Wilson and John Dunn had returned your calls (general queries)

- Valerie Singleton had rung again.

In addition you have the following actions on your daily 'to do' list:

- Ring John Barnes of the ACE Recruitment Agency. They have advertised for a vacancy in the department and are doing a final filter of applicants so that interviews can be arranged.

- You still have to finalise your progress report for your 4.00 pm meeting with your boss. This will take you half an hour.

- You promised, preferably today, to separately see John Holmes and Arthur Kingsley, both department heads, for about half an hour on fact-finding interviews.

- You have also promised your partner that you will be home by 6.00 pm to look after the children for an hour while they attend a PTA meeting. This means leaving the office at 5.30 pm sharp.

You have just completed your initial sift through and the telephone rings. It is Dave Sands, another team manager. He has a small problem and wants to pop round immediately as he thinks you can help. You tell him you can only spare 5 minutes.

It is now 8.55 am and you start to plan out your day. At that moment Jenny Roberts, a junior team member, pokes her head around the door and asks to see you as quickly as possible on a 'personal' matter. Dave Sands is on his way round, you need to plan out the day, what do you say to her? Organise your actions in the form of an activity list with a note of the reasons why you have chosen that particular order.

Suggested solution

When a team member asks for a meeting on a 'personal matter' this has to be treated as urgent and important. With Dave Sands on his way round the best thing to say to Jennie is that Dave is on his way and that you will see her immediately afterwards at 9.15 pm. This also gives a few minutes to quickly outline a plan for the day:

9.00 am   See Dave Sands. Urgent, get it out of the way.

9.15 am   See Jenny Roberts. Urgent and important. Find out what the problem is, and it is usually something that can be sorted out straight away. What is urgent and important to Jennie may not be the same for yourself.

9.30 am   Read appraisal information, internal bulletin. Finalise plan for day.
            Make telephone calls:
                Valerie Singleton – could be course has been cancelled or postponed.
                Holmes/Kingsley – availability for half-hour meetings 12.30, 3.00 pm and 5.00 pm.
                John Barnes – update on recruitment.
                Mrs Wright – confirm arrangements.
                Janet Martin – normally, unless somebody leaves information as to why they are calling, go on the basis that if it is important they will ring again.
            Arrange review with Howard Johnson for 12 noon.
            Prepare for meeting with Stephen Spencer (Personnel).
            Leave office at 10.55 am to get there on time.

11.00 am   Meeting with Stephen Spencer.

12.00 noon Progress review with Howard Johnson.

12.30 pm   Contingency or possible alternative for Holmes/Kingsley meeting.

1.00 pm   Lunch

1.30 pm   Claire Cuthbert, birthday drink. Going at this time ensures that you don't spend too much time in the pub, fulfils your commitment and if you get away just before 2.00 pm will give a little extra preparation time for the team meeting at 2.15 pm.

2.15 pm   Team meeting.

3.00 pm	Contingency Holmes/Kingsley meeting.
3.30 pm	Prepare for review meeting.
4.00 pm	Review meeting with boss.
5.00 pm	Contingency, possible alternative for Holmes/Kingsley meeting.
5.30 pm	Leave for home.

In theory it is possible to get everything in, but in practice

- meetings invariably overrun scheduled times due to poor control
- unscheduled events account for up to 30 per cent of available time
- interruptions can add up to 50 per cent of the normal time needed to do the job.

It is therefore important to set up a time management system that:

- Prioritises and categorises paperwork into appropriate actions to enable you to systematically work through the paperwork. Remember, tidy desks cause less stress!
- Takes into consideration the 80/20 rule:

  80 per cent of time available produces 20 per cent results

  20 per cent of time available produces 80 per cent results.

- Comprises a daily 'to do' list which is visible, prioritised and updated daily:
  – a short-term planner showing the week's actions and appointments
  – a long-term planner to give the long-term overview.

This means that you have to:

- plan and set objectives
- work smarter
- delegate
- differentiate between urgent and important
- run effective meetings.

Time management is a self-discipline. We all have the same amount of time during the working day to get the job done. It is how we use that time that makes us effective at doing our job.

EXERCISE 7 – TEAM PROBLEM-SOLVING

Objective: To reinforce the benefits of solving problems as a team rather than as individuals.
Materials: Problem Solving Questionnaire.
Timing: 45 minutes.

Running the exercise

1. Hand out one copy of the questionnaire to each person and tell them that they have 20 minutes to answer as many questions as possible.

2. After 20 minutes ask each person how many questions they managed to answer. Add them up and divide by the number of persons to get the average.

3. Ask the team to work together for 10 minutes to answer the questions and at the end of that time to tell you how many of the 26 questions have been answered. It will undoubtedly be greater than the average.

4. Finally read out the answers to any incorrect or unanswered questions.

PROBLEM-SOLVING QUESTIONNAIRE

This exercise has been designed to use your knowledge and deductive skills to determine the answers. You have 20 minutes to answer as many questions as you can and they will then be consolidated as a group to give an overall picture.

1. 16   = O in a P
2. 7   = W of the AW
3. 26   = L of the A
4. 1001 = AN
5. 12   = S of the Z
6. 54   = C in a D (with the Js)
7. 9   = P in the SS
8. 88   = PK
9. 13   = S on the AF
10. 32   = DF at which WF
11. 18   = H on a GC
12. 90   = D in a RA
13. 100 = L on a C
14. 200 = P for PG in M
15. 9   = O over the E
16. 4   = Q in a C
17. 24   = H in a D
18. 1   = W on a U
19. 3   = WM (SA, HA, SN)
20. 57   = HV
21. 11   = P in a FT
22. 100 = W that a P is W
23. 29   = D in F in a LY
24. 9   = L of a C
25. 64   = S on a CB
26. 40   = D and N of the GF

PROBLEM SOLVING QUESTIONNAIRE – ANSWERS

1. 16   = Ounces in a Pound
2. 7   = Wonders of the Ancient World
3. 26   = Letters of the Alphabet
4. 1001 = Arabian Nights
5. 12   = Signs of the Zodiac
6. 54   = Cards in a Deck (with the Jokers)
7. 9   = Planets in the Solar System
8. 88   = Piano Keys
9. 13   = Stripes on the American Flag
10. 32   = Degrees Fahrenheit at which Water Freezes
11. 18   = Holes on a Golf Course
12. 90   = Degress in a Right Angle
13. 100 = Legs on a Centipede
14. 200 = Pounds for Passing Go on Monopoly
15. 9   = One over the Eight
16. 4   = Quadrants in a Circle
17. 24   = Hours in a Day
18. 1   = Wheels on a Unicycle
19. 3   = Wise Monkeys (See All, Hear All, Say Nothing)
20. 57   = Heinz Varieties
21. 11   = Players in a Football Team
22. 1000 = Words that a Picture is Worth
23. 29   = Days in February in a Leap Year
24. 9   = Lives of a Cat
25. 64   = Squares on a Chess Board
26. 40   = Days and Nights of the Great Flood

EXERCISE 8 – MULTI-TASK MANAGEMENT

Objectives: To put into practice time management, resource-scheduling, problem-solving, decision-making and team management.

Materials: Task Sheets.
Planning Chart.

Timing: This depends upon the number of tasks that you allocate for the service. Allow 30 minutes for completing each task and 10 minutes feedback per task.

Running the exercise

1. Explain to your team that they will be given a number of tasks to complete within a given time. They must allocate their resources, i.e. people, and plan the time for each task. Initially the team must complete the Planning Chart by listing each task, the names of those people who will be undertaking it and the planned start and finish time. This must be completed and handed to you before they actually begin doing any tasks. When all the tasks have been completed, the team must present their results as required.

2. Give one Task Sheet and one Planning Chart to the team. You may appoint a leader if you wish. Tell the team the total time that they have to plan, complete the tasks and present the results.

3. Finally discuss how the results were achieved, emphasising the positives and looking at ways to overcome the negatives for the future.

MULTI-TASK MANAGEMENT – TASKS TO BE COMPLETED

1. Car park survey 1

It is proposed to redesign the car park taking into consideration the size of vehicles to optimise available parking space. You have been asked to survey existing parking areas and to make recommendations regarding an optimised layout and how it relates to existing car park capacity. The sizes of vehicles to be covered by the survey are:

(a) less than 12 feet

(b) 12–15 feet

(c) over 15 feet.

Resources to be allocated: 2 or more persons. Results to be presented as existing layout and proposed layout.

2. Car park survey 2

You have been asked to undertake a survey of all vehicles parked in the car parks for any half-hour period during normal working hours but not between 12 noon and 2.00 pm. The survey to cover:

(a) total number of vehicles parked

(b) number of vehicles with an out-of-date or non-displayed tax disc

(c) number of vehicles pre-1962/3

(d) number of foreign vehicles

(e) number of vehicles with the latest registration letter

(f) number of vehicles with personalised number plates

(g) number of vehicles by manufacturer.

Resources to be allocated: 2 or more persons. Results to be presented in pie-chart form.

N.B. Even though these two tasks must be kept separate with different task managers the same resources can be used if it is considered an advantage.

3. Traffic survey

You are asked to undertake two traffic surveys for ten-minute periods between the hours of 2.00 and 2.30 pm and 4.30 and 5.00 pm at the junction of ..... and ..... The purpose of the survey is to rearrange the traffic flow/install traffic lights/put in a mini-roundabout/make recommendations regarding pedestrian crossings/cycle and or bus lanes (whichever is most appropriate). You are required to provide the following information:

(a)   the number of pedestrians crossing the road at each point of the junction

(b)   the number of private cars, taxis, vans, lorries, buses, cyclists and motor cyclists entering and leaving by each exit.

Resources to be allocated for each survey – 4 or more persons, not the same people if possible. (Ensure that the junction is busy enough to justify 1 person at each exit.) Results and recommendations to be presented in diagrammatic form with the statistical information on the diagram.

4. Interviewing survey

You have been asked to undertake an interviewing survey within the company covering at least 20 people to establish their method of transport to and from their place of work, improvements that could be made and alternatives they would consider if the facilities were provided. You will need to design a questionnaire and will be required to summarise the findings and to present them to the multi-task manager during the review phase.

Resources to be allocated: 2 or more persons. Results to be presented as a summary of the information gathered on the forms.

N.B. The form and questions can be drawn up in conjunction with the Personnel Department.

5. Garden survey 1

Where a local 'green area' is available the task can be to draw a bird's eye view of a specified area showing:

(a)   the different types of trees within the area

(b)   main shrubs

(c)   wildlife

(d)   other distinctive features.

The task itself can be related to documenting local green areas for conservation purposes. You may also need reference books on trees and shrubs to help get the task done.

Resources to be allocated: 2 or more persons. Results to be presented as a bird's eye view of the area with the names of trees and shrubs on the diagram and a summary of wildlife on the right-hand side of the diagram.

6. Garden survey 2

The same sort of area, but this time it is proposed to convert the area to a 9-hole pitch and putt course. The area will need to have some open spaces with the requirement to remove some trees. The terms of reference to cover:

(a)   Each hole not to be less than 50 yards or more than 80 yards, and not crossing over each other.

(b)   Type, height and main trunk weight of trees to be removed. (The height can be calculated approximately by standing at a distance from the tree and holding a pencil upright at arm's length such that the tree is covered by the pencil, and then turning the pencil horizontal. A person then paces out the pencil length from the base of tree. The height is the number of paces × length of pace.)

(c)   A plan view of the proposed pitch and putt green showing which trees have been removed and those that are remaining.

Resources to be allocated: 2 or more persons. Results presented as bird's eye view of area.

7. Fitness centre

As part of the organisation's plans to provide better facilities for employees, it is proposed to convert an existing area (which you can choose yourself) into a fitness centre. You are required to undertake a survey among your colleagues and as a result recommend the equipment that will be needed, the layout of the equipment (to scale) within the designated area plus any other facilities that may be required such as changing rooms, etc.

Resources to be allocated: 1 or more persons. Results presented as recommendations and scale layout of equipment.

8. Games room

As above except it is proposed to convert the available area into a games room to include:

(a)   a full-size snooker table

(b)   a table tennis table

(c)   darts

(d)   2 PCs for video games, etc.

Resources to be allocated: 1 or more persons. Results presented as recommendations and scale layout of equipment.

Other tasks can cover:
*   buildings survey, converting to/from open plan
*   cost of exterior glass cleaning based on £x per square foot
*   volume of paint required to paint a nominated building to a thickness of 1 mm
*   street interviewing survey, etc.

All tasks should be interesting, achievable and where possible have a reason for being done.

Planning Chart

Activity	Resources	Timescales						

Appendix 2
Answers to Exercises

CHAPTER 2

Exercise 1

- **Nigel** is using the Tell style of leadership which is quite common with task-oriented managers.

    In the circumstances it would be more appropriate if he adopted a Test or Consult style to give his team the opportunity to suggest ways of achieving the increase in revenue. Even if they ended up with Nigel's suggestion, they would feel more committed having had the chance to air their views.

- Although **Sue** has plenty of ideas of her own, she has used the Consult style which is quite appropriate in this case.

- **Tom** has used the Tell style to select the team. Because he does not yet know the abilities of his players this is probably the most sensible approach. Whilst team selection is his responsibility, in the future he should give reasons for his selection by using the Sell style.

CHAPTER 5

Identifying communication behaviours (page 50).

1. proposing

2. testing understanding

3. blocking

4. seeking information

5. supporting

6. building

7. proposing

8. giving information

9. summarising

10. shutting out/attacking

11. clarifying

12. bringing in

13. disagreeing

14. harmonising

15. attacking

16. open

Glossary

Assessment. Review of team's performance.

Assertiveness. Clearly stating one's rights or opinions without emotion.

Behaviour. Way in which people react to given situations.

Body language. Gestures and postures which reveal a person's feelings and emotions.

Brainstorm. Method of involving groups of people in solving problems by encouraging everyone to offer ideas and suggestions and writing them down on a flipchart, whiteboard or similar, initially without discussion, comment or judgement.

Communication. The exchange of ideas or information between groups or individuals to achieve a mutual understanding.

Decision. Making a choice between two or more options.

Delegation. The passing over of a task and/or responsibility to another person.

Exercise. Aid to team training.

Grievance. Dispute between two or more people.

Group. A collection or assembly of people.

Incentive. A reward offered for performing specific tasks.

Innovation. Making changes, introducing new ideas, methods or practices.

Leader. One who leads a team of people

Leadership. The act of leading.

Leadership styles. Methods of leading or managing depending upon the situation or people involved.

Motivate. Offering the appropriate incentives to satisfy individuals' needs in return for achieving specific targets or behaving in the required manner.

Objectives. Targets or goals that can be quantified.

Problems. Questions or situations which require a solution.

Quantifiable. Able to be measured in physical terms, e.g. costs, revenue, time.

Recognition. The level of quality, performance, discipline and so on to which others should perform.

Stress. A mental state brought about by excessive pressure at work and/or at home.

Target. A group of people working together to achieve a specific objective.

Team. A group of people working together to achieve a specific objective.

Teambuilding. The moulding of a group into a team.

Teamworking. The combined actions of a team especially when effective and efficient.

Training. The process of teaching a skill or method.

Further Reading

GENERAL

How To Be an Even Better Manager, Michael Armstrong (Kogan Page 4th edition 1998).
Managing Through People, John Humphries (How To Books 3rd edition 1998).

COMMUNICATION

Body Language, Alan Pease (Sheldon Press 1981).
How To Communicate at Work, Ann Dobson (How To Books 1994).
Understanding Body Language, Jane Lyle (Hamlyn 1989).

LEADERSHIP

The Discipline of Real Leadership in the Workplace, Edward Handyside (Gower 1997).
Leadership, James G Hunt (Sage 1991).

TEAMWORK

Building a Better Team, Peter Moxon (Gower 1998).
Successful Teambuilding in a Week, Graham Wilcocks and Steve Morris (Hodder & Stoughton 1995).
Teamwork – Key Issues, Campell Ford (ACAS 1994).
Teamwork – New Management Ideas for the 90s, D. Petersen and J. Hillkirk (Gollancz 1991).
The Teamwork Pocketbook, Ian Fleming (Melrose 1996).
Teamwork Success Through People, ACAS (ACAS 1996).

TRAINING

Team Development Games for Trainers, Roderick Stuart (Gower

1998).

The Techniques of Training, Leslie Rae (Gower 3rd edition 1995).

PRACTICAL EXERCISES FOR TEAM TRAINING

Contact Training Consultancy Services, 9 Sherwood Drive, Maidenhead, Berks SL6 4NY. Tel: (01628) 621425.

Index

assertiveness, 52
assessing teams, 71
assessing training, 68

benefiting from teams, 12
body language, 52
bonding, 44
brainstorming, 41
brainwriting, 42
building teams, 34

case studies, 14, 26, 36, 44, 55, 62, 69, 73
clarifying objectives, 40
communication, 46
communication barriers, 47
communication behaviours, 48
communication purposes, 46
conflict, causes of, 57
conflict, dealing with, 59
creating the right environment, 39

delegating, 23
directing, 23

earning respect, 19
exercises, 27, 50
exercises, answers, 108
external training, 64

forming, 34

giving instructions, 53
groups, defining, 11

information, sharing, 40
internal training, 65
involving, 41, 72

leading by example, 40
leadership, 16
leadership demands, 20
leadership, influences on, 25
leadership qualities, 17
leadership responsibilities, 19
leadership, situational, 24
leadership styles, 21
listening skills, 54

meetings, 43
monitoring performance, 71
movitation, 40

norming, 35

people orientated leaders, 21
performing, 35

resources, 29

storming, 35
strengths and weaknesses, 30
successful teams, 11
supporting, 23

task orientated leaders, 21
teambuilding, 28
teambuilding, objectives, 28
team exercises, 75
team roles, 32
teams, defining, 11
teams, types of, 13
teamworking, 38
teamworking, benefits of, 39

tone, 51
training, 42, 64
training, delivering, 67
training, need, 66
training, planning, 67
training records, 68
training, types of, 64

words, 51

MANAGING THROUGH PEOPLE
How to get the best from your most valuable resource

John Humphries

People are the most valuable resource of any organisation, and managing people successfully is the surest way for an organisation to achieve its objectives. *Managing Through People*, originally titled *How To Manage People at Work*, has been fully revised to take into account the changing role of managers, for example how to support and coordinate a non-standard workforce, such as those working from home on a freelance basis. In fact this book covers, in one handy volume, every aspect of people management that today's business leaders require. 'Highly informative, reliable, comprehensive and user-friendly – has tackled an extremely wide subject ably and well.' *Progress* (NEBS Management Association). John Humphries BSc has 20 years' professional experience as a management trainer and is an NVQ assessor.

128pp illus. 1 85703 271 3. 3rd edition.

MANAGING YOURSELF
How to achieve your personal goals at work

Julie-Ann Amos

Managing yourself is often more difficult than it seems. This simple book goes beyond assertiveness and behaviour, and examines how to deal inside ourselves with the conflicts of everyday life. The reader will learn how to handle criticism, thoughts and emotions, aggression, passivity, change, conflict, and stress, through developing assertive communication and listening skills, body language and confidence.

160pp. illus. 1 85703 324 8.

ORGANISING EFFECTIVE TRAINING
How to play and run successful courses and seminars

James Chalmers

This book explains how to plan and organise really successful training events. The method can be applied to anything, from team building to technical courses, and from a one hour briefing up to events lasting several days. The step-by-step approach is easy to follow, and will work as well with organisers who are unfamiliar with the subject to be trained, as it will with professional trainers.

160pp. illus. 1 85703 329 9.

CONDUCTING STAFF APPRAISALS
A practical handbook for every manager today

Nigel Hunt

This book, now in a third edition, sets out a basic framework which every manager can use or adapt, whether in business and industry, transport, education, health or public services. Nigel Hunt is a consultant in occupational testing, selection, appraisal, vocational assessment, and management development. He is a Graduate Member of the British Psychological Society, and Associate Member of the Institute of Personnel & Development. 'Informative. . .. points for discussion and case studies are prominent throughout. . . the case studies are highly relevant and good.' *Progress* (NEBS Management Association Journal). 'Not all books live up to their promises. This one does. At the price it is a bargain.' *British Journal of Administrative Management.*

154pp illus. 1 85703 399 X. 3rd edition.

HOW TO COMMUNICATE AT WORK
Making a success of your working relationships

Ann Dobson

This very practical step-by-step guide gets to the very basics of good communication: how to speak and listen, how to ask and answer questions, how to take messages and use the telephone, how to liaise, negotiate, persuade, offer advice and accept criticism, how to stand up for yourself, dealing with shyness, a difficult boss or angry customer, how to use and understand body language properly, how to cope with visitors, how to store and present information – and a great deal more.

192pp illus. 1 85703 103 2.

WRITING A REPORT
A step-by-step guide to effective report writing

John Bowden

Written by an experienced manager and staff trainer, this well-presented handbook provides a clear step-by-step framework for every individual, whether dealing with professional colleagues, customers, clients, suppliers of junior or senior staff. Contents include: preparation and planning, collecting and handling information, writing the report, improving your thinking and presentation, achieving a good writing style, making effective use of English, and how to choose illustrations, paper, covers and binding. Thoroughly commendable.' *IPS Journal.* John Bowden MSc has long experience both as a professional manager in industry, and as a Senior Lecturer running courses in accountancy, auditing and effective communication.

215pp illus. 1 85703 285 3. 4th edition.

PREPARING A BUSINESS PLAN
How to lay the right foundations for business success

Matthew Record

A business plan is the most important commercial document you will ever have to produce, whether you are just starting out in business, or are already trading. A well thought out and carefully structured plan will be crucial to the survival and long-term success of the enterprise. Poor planning has been identified as the major cause of business failure. With the odds so stacked against success, make sure YOUR business gets off to the right start. Matthew Record is a business consultant specialising in the preparation of business plans for a variety of commercial clients. His company, Phoenix Business Plans, is based in Dorset.

158pp illus. 1 85703 374 4. 2nd edition.

WRITING BUSINESS LETTERS
How to tackle your day-to-day business correspondence successfully

Ann Dobson

Intended for absolute beginners, this book uses fictional characters in a typical business setting to contrast the right and wrong ways to go about things. Taking nothing for granted, the book shows: how to plan a letter, how to write and present it, how to deal with requests, how to write and answer complaints, standard letters, personal letters, job applications, letters overseas, and a variety of routine and tricky letters. Good, bad and middling examples are used to help beginners see for themselves the right and wrong ways of doing things. Ann Dobson is Principal of a secretarial training school with long experience of helping people improve their business skills.

183pp illus. 1 85703 339 6. 2nd edition.

MAKING EFFECTIVE SPEECHES
How to motivate and persuade in every business situation

John Bowden

Written specifically for people competing in today's tough business world, this book shows you how to get that competitive edge by becoming a comfortable, effective speaker, equipped with the skills necessary to deliver dynamic business speeches. You will learn how to communicate your ideas, motivate employees, influence opinions, and much more. Business speeches are important – they must succeed. This book will help turn your speeches into personal and corporate triumphs. John Bowden MSc has over 25 years' experience as a manager in industry, and as a professional trainer and senior lecturer in communication skills. He is author of *Making a Wedding Speech* and *Writing a Report* in this series.

144pp. 1 85703 291 8.

MANAGING YOUR TIME
What to do and how to do it in order to do more

Julie-Ann Amos

Time cannot be managed. It can't be increased, delegated, reallocated, saved, or lost. What you can manage is the way you use time. This practical guide looks at the two issues of what you do and how you do it. Doing the right things in the best way means we can use our time to our best advantage – efficiently. You will learn the difference between efficiency and effectiveness, and how to use them to make time your friend, not your enemy. Julie-Ann Amos BSc holds post-graduate qualifications and memberships of the Institutes of Personnel Development and Administrative Management. She works as a human resources consultant with a number of public and private sector companies.

128pp. illus. 1 85703 288 8.